It's Not Just about the Boxes

SEVEN SIMPLE STEPS TO A SUCCESSFUL MOVE

America's Relocation Specialist
Laura Ackerman

Published by
RockStar Publishing House
32129 Lindero Canyon Road, Suite 205
Westlake Village, CA 91361
www.rockstarpublishinghouse.com

Manufactured in the United States of America, or in the United Kingdom when distributed elsewhere.

Ackerman, Laura
It's Not Just About The Boxes
Paperback: 9781937506933
eBook: 9781937506940

Cover design by: Tim Durning
Cover photo by: Kelle Mac Photography
Interior design: Jason Hughes
Photo credits: Kelle Mac Photography

http://www.americasrelocationspecialist.com/

To my parents, Kenneth and Janice, who gave me unconditional love and confidence

---

To my husband, Don, who gave me his heart and a life full of adventure

---

To my sons, Adam and Andrew, who gave me the greatest blessings of motherhood and always displayed great strength by stepping out of the box

Contents

Step 4: *Saying Your Good-Byes*

Introduction

As I look around my house full of moving boxes and disassembled furniture, I once again muse, "Here we go again!" How did I end up in this life of relocations? The first twenty-three years of my life had been spent at the exact same address. Now after thirty years of marriage, I look back at a life full of moving boxes! It's hard to believe that my husband and I have just purchased our ninth home, on top of experiencing several temporary living addresses. How did this happen to a simple girl from Evansville, Indiana, who never planned to leave her hometown? I had never packed more than a simple suitcase to go anywhere but to venture on our annual family vacation to Daytona Beach, Florida! Now I am packing entire homes, children, pets, and vehicles and moving all the way across the country.

Over the years, I have figured out that there is so much more to a move than boxes, trucks, and aching backs. It's much deeper than that. In fact, I personally believe that moving is only 30% about the boxes and 70% about emotion. A move involves relationships, change, unfamiliarity, blind faith, loneliness, excitement, and personal growth. It's not just the "stuff" we put into boxes and unpack at our new location. It's a journey that impacts our lives and our loved ones in many ways.

Looking back over the years, I can recall driving into one of our new neighborhoods and wondering what life would bring us at this new home. Even though we did not know anyone, I did know that God would provide for all our needs. Years later, as we pulled away from our sold home, I looked back in the rearview mirror and felt blessed for the memories we had acquired—lifelong friendships that were gained, teachers who had a positive influence on my children, career experience that flourished, and faith that grew even deeper through trusting in God's plan.

As America's Relocation Specialist, I know that you may be having many doubts about your upcoming move. Do you stay in your comfort zone, or do you take a step into the unknown world of possibilities? I always tell my clients, "If you don't go, you will never know!" Whether you are moving across the street or across the nation, this book will help guide you through the stress and disorganization of your relocation.

While I will be focusing more on long-distance moves, several of the concepts will apply to local moves. I tell my clients to be prepared to wear many "hats" throughout this process. You will take on the role of a project manager, administrative assistant, accountant, logistics specialist, customer service representative, and psychiatrist! You will master the art of multitasking! I will provide you my insight and some easy-to-follow tips that will help guide you as you make decisions to plan, organize, and execute this very exciting adventure.

Step 1

It's Your Move

Making the Decision

The first step that I would like to discuss is the decision you will need to make as to whether you should move. Whether you are moving as a single person or as an entire family, this decision can be tough. It is important that you dedicate time to fully evaluating the pros and cons of your decision. You need to feel confident that you have made the best choice. I warn my clients that once the moving announcements begin and the world is full of questions, it will be important for them to feel comfortable with their decision, knowing that they made the best decision based on the information they have at this time. Regardless of the "static" or judgment that you may receive from your friends, family, and significant others, you will be able to confidently stand firm.

More than thirty years ago, my husband and I stood before two hundred people and vowed that for better or for worse, for richer or for poorer, we were committed to form a union of three: husband, wife, and our God. As with any newlyweds, we had many hopes and dreams for our future. Looking back, I see that out of the many blessings that our parents gave us, one of their greatest gifts was the gift of independence. At a time when they wanted to hold on tight, they released us to make decisions as husband and wife regarding every aspect of our life, including our numerous relocations. It was important to our marriage that we made these moving decisions together, especially when it came time for career advancements, job security, and taking responsibility for our family.

Big decisions can cause serious stress in your life. One of the toughest decisions is to leave your closest family and friends. To think that you won't have daily contact can be heartbreaking. A decision of this type will require you to stick to your guns by evaluating the black-and-white facts while attempting to leave your emotions on the back doorstep. Your decision regarding this move will serve as the first brick in the foundation of this relocation. As you journey down this road, you will be faced with many options, and at times the pressure of making all the right decisions will feel overwhelming. Whether you are purchasing a home, selecting a new school, or simply cleaning out a cabinet, I am providing some decision-making tools that may be helpful to this process.

Listing the Pros and Cons

In what follows, I have listed several questions that you may want to consider when listing your pros and cons. These questions will help you dive deeper into your thought process as well as include those significant others who will be directly involved in your decision to relocate. As you ponder the pros and cons, rank each one on a scale of 1–10, with 1 being the least important and 10 being the most important.

Is This Move Necessary for Career Growth?

Some career credentials can only be acquired with hands-on experience. If you can't get the necessary experience locally, then it may be necessary to move to where you can gain experience. Textbook or academic training cannot replace real-world experience.

Is This a Job Growth Experience?

As you advance in your career, the availability of upper level positions starts to decline. Gaining experience in an industry can sometimes be more valuable in the short term than gaining income. Ideally, you can gain both.

Will It Be a Career-Limiting Move If You Decide to Decline This Relocation?

In this dog-eat-dog world of corporate America, you may only be offered this opportunity once. In my experience, I have found that once you notify your company that you are unwilling to relocate, the company will move on to someone who will be willing to relocate.

Is Your Spouse or Significant Other "On Board" with This Big Life Transition?

The ideal situation is that your spouse or significant other will support you on this decision to relocate. Everyone involved in this decision will experience a great deal of stress, sadness, and anxiety. The likelihood of success will be much greater if you can all work as a team. You are setting yourself up for failure if your significant other refuses to go or their family is determined to make everything about the relocation difficult. This could be a deal-breaker if you don't have their support.

On the flip side, are you going to hold grudges against your loved ones because they held you back from a brighter career opportunity? This is a very important discussion for everyone involved in this relocation. This is where the terms *give* and *take* come into a relationship. I can recall talking with an older man about his marriage of sixty years. I asked him how he and his wife were able to have a successful marriage. He said, "It's simple. I give and she takes!"

Are You Unemployed and Have You Acquired a Job in a New Location?

With the economic downturn of the early millennium, unemployment has been high for several years. With ongoing corporate downsizings, the job market has become flooded with an abundance of qualified applicants. Sometimes there is no choice but to move to where you can gain employment.

Is This a "Faith-Based" Move?

In the book *The Purpose Driven Life*, Rick Warren talks about the fact that we were born by God's purpose and for God's purpose. Through prayer and obedience, some people feel called to relocate as a part of God's purpose for their lives.

Can You Afford This Move or Will This Move Be Financially Beneficial?

When we were asked to move from Tennessee to California, we became concerned about our ability to afford the higher cost of living. It is important to consider the various costs involved with the relocation and ensure that you are making a wise decision.

- Does your salary reflect the increase or decrease in the cost of living?

- How is the benefits package (medical and dental insurance, life insurance, vacation days, holidays, etc.)?
- To what extent will your company reimburse you for moving expenses?
- Will you be reimbursed for closing costs and realtor fees?
- Will your children be able to attend public schools or will you be paying private tuition?
- How difficult will it be for your significant other to acquire a job?
- What lifestyle adjustments will be required?
- Do you have children getting ready to attend an in-state college? Will their tuition costs be affected?
- Will you be able to afford plane tickets and travel expenses to visit family?

What Is Your Moving Experience?

If you have never relocated out of town, then you will be stepping way outside your comfort zone. It is only natural to experience some overwhelming fears of the unknown. If you have relocated before, then you already have an idea of what may be ahead of you. Sometimes a new career opportunity, the adventure of new surroundings, and the potential for personal growth can be exciting. The newness of everything can rejuvenate your life as a whole. You will find that the more moving experience you gain, the more efficient you become in your expectations of resettling. In the next section, I will discuss whether it is time for a change.

Why Should You *Not* Move?

Certain extenuating circumstances may make it tough to relocate at this time. The following are some items that you may need to consider:

- care of an elderly parent
- disabilities or special needs
- medical care, such as for established cancer treatments or a difficult pregnancy
- your spouse or significant other being unable to relocate due to a booming career
- children who are in their senior year of high school or completing a degree

Listing the pros and cons is one way to thoroughly evaluate a decision to ensure that the best action is taken. To further assist you,

I have listed some additional tips that my clients have found helpful when determining the best decision.

- What advice would you give your friend if he or she approached you with this decision? Forget for the moment that this is your life. Looking in from the outside will eliminate clouding of judgment with emotion.
- Discuss this decision with an intelligent and trusted friend, relative, or advisor who will not allow their personal emotions to get involved. I have found that the fewer people are involved in this decision, the fewer opinions and confusion you will experience.
- Tell yourself for a moment that this opportunity is clearly impossible and that this relocation would never be successful. Somewhere deep down, do you feel this move could be possible? Then, pretending that you have said yes to this decision, ask yourself exactly how you would do it.
- Ask yourself, "What is the worst thing that can happen if we move?" Maybe down the road you will determine that you made the wrong decision. Cross that bridge when you come to it. Decisions are based on the information in the present, and no one has the power to see the future. As hard as we try in life, circumstances are always changing, and it is not possible to make the "perfect" decision for everyone involved and in every situation.
- Go for a walk and have some quiet time so that your unconscious mind can work. Sometimes it works best to sleep on big decisions. Your outlook may be different after a good night's sleep.

Every day we make hundreds of small decisions without blinking an eye, but major, life-changing decisions, like moving to another city, can weigh heavily on our emotions. While it is good to objectively document the black-and-white facts about a decision, at the end of the day, your instincts can be quite powerful. As a relocation coach, I ask my clients, "Is your heart, head, and gut all balanced with this decision? Do your instincts tell you that your emotions, wisdom, and overall personal insights are evenly aligned with this decision?" If there is conflict in these three areas, then you may want to reconsider your decision.

Is It Time for a Change?

The definition of the word *change* is "to make or become different." People avoid change either because they don't know that they need to change or because they just don't have the motivation to do it. Change can cause people discomfort, and as human beings, we strive to avoid discomfort. We want to stay comfortable in what is familiar and safe. We fear the unknown.

Change is a crucial part of life and important for growth. Steve Jobs once said, "I have looked in the mirror every morning and asked myself: If today were the last day of my life, would I want to do what I am about to do today? And whenever the answer has been 'No' for too many days in a row, I know I need to change something." Change involves personal motivation, goals, and the willingness to stand up against the fear of the unknown. If you are willing to open your mind and heart to something new, a whole world of adventure can be ahead of you.

We are living in the era of "reinvention." While previous generations worked the same job until they retired, the baby boomer generation retires later in life without the same job stability opportunities. We want to be promoted and challenged and continue to grow without getting in a daily rut. This reminds me of the 1993 comedy *Groundhog Day*. Bill Murray finds himself in a time loop, repeating the same daily routine again and again, and remarks, "Well, what if there is no tomorrow? There wasn't one today." Reinvention allows us to reexamine our lives and priorities. Change can be good.

The decision to move is going to be a big change. I tell my clients that just like everything else in life, they will have good days and bad days. Moving to a new home will require day-to-day life adjustments. These adjustments will cause stress, even when the adjustments are positive. This is a good time for you to take some time to fully understand how change will affect your attitude.

An Attitude Adjustment

All those affected by your relocation will have their ups and downs and will be looking to you for guidance. Your perspective will directly affect everyone else's point of view. I realize that talking about attitude doesn't sound anything like packing boxes, but over the next several months, you will be amazed how much your mind-set influences this experience. Before you start announcing this decision, take a look at your attitude.

It will be necessary to maintain a **positive attitude** in every aspect of this move. As Winston Churchill once said, "The pessimist sees the difficulty in every opportunity; an optimist sees the opportunity in every difficulty." The power of positive thinking doesn't mean that you keep your head in the sand and ignore all the difficulties of this relocation. Positive thinking and self-talk will allow you to think the best is going to happen, not the worst.

Studies have proven the numerous health benefits of how a **happy attitude** allows people the ability to better cope during times of hardship and stress. The one-hit wonder Bobby McFerrin snapped, popped, and sang into fame with the song "Don't Worry, Be Happy." The whole premise of this upbeat song is that in everyday life, we will have some trouble, but when you worry, you will make your troubles double. Basically, in life, nothing will ever go as planned. Go with the flow and hold on for the ride of your life. "Don't worry, be happy!"

I have found with all our relocations that I needed to stay grounded with a **faithful attitude**. I know that God has a plan for all our lives, and we can either go with His plan or fight His plan. "For I know the plans I have for you, plans to prosper you and not harm you, plans to give you hope and a future" (Jeremiah 29:11). While surrendering to God's plan can make us feel "out of control," it is that blind faith that provides us with peace and serenity. There is great power in surrendering.

Another key is a **prayerful attitude**. We should never underestimate the power of prayer. When we pray, we should hold tight to our faith no matter how tough the circumstances. God most definitely listens to our prayers, answers prayers, and moves in response to prayers. While answers never seem to come quick enough for us, I know we must wait on the Lord and let Him answer our prayers in His perfect timing. One of my favorite quotes of Joyce Meyer is "God may not be early, but he will never be late."

A **patient attitude** is a virtue; as the old English proverb states, "All good things come to those who wait." While you may feel overwhelmed right now, remember the relocation process is not a race but a marathon. Remind yourself to take one day at a time. Let those around you adjust to this process at their own rate. Be patient with all the people with whom you will be working, including realtors, moving companies, leasing agents, Internet service providers, and so on. Not everyone will have your same sense of urgency. With one of our most recent relocations, our family was required to wait ten weeks to acquire Internet service in our new home. How do you live without Gmail, Facebook, Google, or the visual discovery tool of Pinterest?

An **empathetic attitude** will be necessary in order for you to recognize and share emotions experienced by all those loved ones around you. One of your children may be happily sitting in the car ready to go, while your other child may be locked in her bedroom crying and refusing to move. One moment your spouse may be upbeat and onboard with the move, and then in the next moment he may be depressed and down in the dumps about leaving his previous life.

A **flexible attitude** may be the most important of all. The proverbial expression "Even the best laid plans" signifies the futility of making detailed plans when the outcome is uncertain. I have always liked the saying "If you want to see God laugh, have a plan!" The point is that you need to go with the flow. I tell my clients to expect appointments to change, workers not to show, items to break, flat tires to occur, and possibly even a case of chicken pox to be diagnosed! Find some humor in the moment, laugh, and adjust your plan accordingly.

The Moving Announcement

Telling the Children

The time has come to talk with your children about your decision to move. You have spent several days contemplating, discussing, and preparing yourself for this next step. I feel that telling the children is the most difficult. Maybe it's because you can so easily remember what it was like to be a child. Maybe it's because we never want our children to endure pain and unhappiness.

Over the years of raising our two boys, we were required to have this talk numerous times. Regardless of their ages, it never got any easier. Although, while we automatically think that this announcement will be taken badly, sometimes children see it as a good thing. I know that there were times when our older son Adam was actually happy to hear that we were moving. He was excited to think he would be able to move into a new house, make some new friends, eat at some new restaurants, and get some new teachers!

I warn my clients that regardless of the response, they will need to be prepared to answer a lot of questions while remaining open to whatever emotions are expressed. Remember that you have already had the opportunity to process and mentally prepare yourself. Your children will need some time, too. Be positive, wear your heart on your sleeve, and most of all, stay upfront and honest.

The following are some questions that my children asked when we made the moving announcement.

- Why do we have to move?
- When did you decide that we were going to move?
- Can we just stay here and let Dad move for now?
- Will we have to go to a new school?
- Why do we have to leave our friends?
- Will Grandma and Grandpa come visit us?
- Where will we live?
- Can we move back if we don't like it?
- When are we moving?

On our most recent move, our younger son, Andrew, was just completing eighth grade. He had spent three years of middle school building friendships and looking forward to his high school years. We decided to talk with Andrew about the move on a Saturday so that he would have some time to ponder the announcement without having to focus on school. As we sat eating lunch with Andrew, we told him our story about our decision to move from California to Georgia. We expressed our faith and that we knew that God would be in control of this situation. The deeper we went into the story, the more tears began to build in his eyes. We felt terrible. We hurt for him. We didn't want to bring this pain into his life. We paused and sat quietly while we waited for his response.

Andrew's initial response was that he was not going to move. He wanted to stay where he was comfortable. He didn't want to go to a new school. He didn't want to start all over again making new friends. From previous experiences, he knew the difficulty of the road ahead of him. Andrew just didn't want to talk about it anymore.

As the days progressed, we started selling him on the upside of moving to Georgia. We didn't force it on him but just kept dropping positive statements. We tried to get him involved as quickly as possible with decisions surrounding the move. We let him pick the school he liked best. We let him pick the room he liked best in our new house. We let him have control over the things that he could control.

Moving is one of the toughest experiences that children can experience. It will be your job to show them that along with the sadness they will experience a lot of happiness in their new home. Studies have shown that no matter the circumstances, if children feel loved, safe, and secure, they can endure some of the toughest experiences in life. Of course, several trips to Toys "R" Us or Best Buy are helpful, too! Our motto is to just "do whatever it takes!"

Looking back over the years and our numerous moves, I have seen my children benefit from being placed into many new situations. While it is never easy, and usually quite painful, the life lessons gained have been irreplaceable. I have always wanted to give my children the gift of "wings." While I would love to hold my children tight with me forever, I know that they, too, will need to take their lives and careers wherever God calls for them to accomplish their purpose.

Telling the Family

One of the saddest days of my life was telling my parents that we would be leaving my hometown. I had lived my entire life on the same street, in the same city, with the exact same routines for twenty-three years. My life was surrounded with two older brothers, a younger sister, childhood friends, family, and 100% familiarity. Why would I want to leave home?

My dreams were that my children would be raised with their grandparents and our holidays would be spent in our home. I wanted my children to wake on Christmas morning in their own bed and run to find that Santa Claus had delivered presents under their own tree. I wanted my family to be able to come to my children's sporting events and school carnivals. I dreamed that my children would have the same hometown, family-focused life that I had experienced.

Another one of the saddest days of my life was when we had to tell our recently married son Adam and his wife, Anna, that we were going to be moving two thousand miles across the country. My heart still hurts thinking about that very painful announcement. To add to Adam's pain was the fact that we were selling the house that he called home. We were also taking his younger brother, Andrew, and his golden retriever, Abbey.

How do you find the strength to make such difficult decisions and announcements? How do you look forward and not look back with regret? How do you board an airplane with your husband, son, and a few pieces of luggage and fly to a place that is 100% unfamiliar? My only answer is that I gain a great amount of peace surrendering my life to God and following the plan that He has placed upon my life.

As I look back over the last thirty years of my "relocation" experiences, I can see some of the greatest blessings that I have received that would have been missed if I had not been willing to walk in "blind faith." I would have missed meeting some of the best friends of my life. I would have missed living in some of the most comfortable homes and seeing some of the most beautiful scenery. Adam, our oldest son, would not have graduated from the University of Tennessee, where he met his amazing wife, Anna. As sad as it has been to sacrifice the plans that I had made for my life, God has given me a life that I never thought was possible for me to plan. I know that "I can do all things through Christ who gives me strength."

Telling your parents and your children that you will be leaving them is just downright sad and scary. But if you don't go, you will never know the many blessings that lie ahead for all of you.

Giving Notice to Employers

There are usually three steps involved in taking a new job with a different company. The first step is to receive the formal job offer. The second step is negotiating and accepting the job offer. The third step is giving notice to your current employer. Once these steps have occurred, dates can be set for the final day at your current employer followed by a date to be set for the first day at your new employer. To keep things running smoothly, it is important that confidentiality be maintained throughout this entire time frame. The last thing you want is to have someone spill the beans based on secondhand gossip.

If you are taking a new position and relocating with your current employer, then decisions and assignment dates will be made internally. This usually runs more smoothly, mainly because you are dealing with the same human resources, benefits, and management departments.

If both husband and wife have careers, your timeline will need to be adjusted so that both announcements will occur simultaneously. I have always wanted to work as long as possible prior to leaving my job to relocate with my husband. While I was able to transfer with my company on several occasions, a timeline of events is important. There are so many factors to consider within the moving timeline. It is always nice if your employer will let you stay on board until your home has sold, children have finished a school year, or another employee has been hired and trained to take your place.

A logistical challenge that we seem to face on every move is the "start date" of the new job. Don's new job always seems to require him to assume his new position ASAP! What that means for him is that he will be traveling once he has completed his final day at his previous job. What that means for me is that I will be in charge of the move. This is how I gained the title "America's Relocation Specialist"! This is why I have written this book and developed my Moving Management System. My biggest suggestion, from my own personal experience, is not to get too far ahead and become overwhelmed. Keep focused on one step at a time, because this exciting ride will be a marathon and not a sprint. Hold on tight!

Spreading the Word

I tell my clients that timing is the most challenging part of telling everyone else about their move. These loved ones deserve the same delicate conversation that you have given your children and your family. No one wants to hear this news second hand, although this kind of information is difficult for people not to want to share with others. Between mobile phones, texting, e-mails, and social media, this announcement can go viral quickly. Before you know it, you have some very dear family and friends with some very hurt feelings. This will cause you to move into damage control mode, and the entire burden of the relocation becomes that much heavier.

My preference has always been to tell people in person. I just think it is impersonal to tell close friends this big news in a telephone call or text. Although, sometimes between the job offer and the announcement, things can move along so quickly that there just isn't enough time for you to handle this announcement the way you would prefer. It can be difficult to track down people in their busy schedules and find enough time to have this heartfelt conversation. Therefore, after several experiences of making "The Moving Announcement," we have determined that we do the best we can with the circumstances we have been given. Meet with those people who are available, call others on the telephone, and send a mass e-mail to all your family, friends, and everyone else involved.

On our most recent move from California to Georgia, I found it most timely to send an e-mail to our family and friends located in various states around the country. I have included a version of this e-mail message in this book to give you an example of an announcement.

Hello Family and Friends:

We are excited to announce that we are going to be moving to Georgia. Don has gained some great job experience here in California and has been recruited to join an even larger company based in Atlanta.

We are in the process of selling our home and making moving arrangements, and we will soon be traveling to Georgia to find a new home. Andrew will finish his eighth grade year here in California before moving to Atlanta at the beginning of the summer. We will keep you posted as we gain more information.

Please keep us in your prayers as we take our next journey of "blind faith." It always feels like we are stepping off of the side of a mountain when we surrender to God's plan! There are always a lot of peaks and valleys throughout this difficult process! We will keep you up-to-date as we keep moving along with our newest "Ackerman Adventure"!

Love, Don, Laura, and Andrew

Another tough step is when your children need to tell their friends about the move. Both Adam and Andrew were concerned about what to say and how their friends would respond. Things become "real" when the words are verbalized, and sometimes emotions can catch you off guard.

In order to help this situation run more smoothly, I first call the mother of each of the closest friends. I give the mother the details of the situation and ask for her to talk with her child. This method allows the friends to get the full details at home rather than in passing on the playground. This will also take a big burden off your children. Once the closest friends are told, they are more prepared to support your children when the moving subject is brought up in a larger group of kids.

I also encourage my clients to e-mail teachers, coaches, and other important figures so that they will be in tune with the situation. They too can provide support and encouragement to your children.

Everyone's Response

So what kind of response should you expect from your moving announcement?

You should expect a lot of questions and a lot of telephone calls! In fact, you won't be able to fully focus on your actual move for a few days, because you will be spending a lot of time telling your story. How long do you think it will take to sell your house? How do the kids feel about leaving their friends? When does your husband start his new job? What date will you be moving? The problem is that people have a lot of questions and you don't have a lot of answers. People want information, but at this point, you really don't have many details.

I warn my clients that some people will doubt their decision. It is easy for people to sit back and judge a decision when they aren't the one living the decision. When you are confronted with doubt, remember to stand firm and confident in your choice. You have already committed your heart and soul to this decision and know that it was not taken lightly.

Not to be negative, but I have always been surprised by the lack of support and encouragement I have received surrounding our moving decisions. There are times that I feel I have spent more time in defense than offense! People seem to focus more on what their life is going to look like once you are gone instead of looking at how difficult your life is going to be all alone. I warn my clients about this possibility just so they can be aware that everyone will respond differently and that sometimes people's responses can catch them off guard.

Over the years, I have found that I prefer not to make our moving announcement too early, because I want to remain active in relationships and social events. I know this sounds odd, but I actually have seen people withdrawal from me the minute they hear I am leaving. It's almost like they implement a self-defense mechanism to emotionally protect themselves. It's strange, but I have seen this happen every time we move.

My son came home from school one day following our announcement and said that he was ready to go ahead with our move. His friends were making plans for the summer, and he felt he no longer seemed to be a part of the equation. All their plans didn't include him, and this made him feel like he had already left. I have had situations where I am not included in a lunch or an activity. Friends may call another friend to help them with something that I would usually do. I don't think people do this to be hurtful; I think they are subconsciously going on with the adjustment process even before the actual departure.

As you continue this journey, you may consider what support you will need from your family and friends. Just like any other major life event, people want to help, but they just don't know how to help. It is very difficult for people to understand every aspect of relocating if they have never experienced it. You will need to tell them specifically what you need from them. Ask for their prayers. Ask for help with your children. Ask for help preparing your home to be sold. If you don't ask, you may not receive what you need the most!

Step 2

Planning, Organizing, and Selling

Moving Management

At this time, I know you are feeling overwhelmed by your long "to do" list. This is the time to develop a manageable plan that can effectively keep you administratively coordinated throughout the moving process. I cannot stress enough the importance of being organized at this time. Lack of organization will cause you frustration, stress, and even money. The process of moving is like running a business, and the more effectively it operates, the more successful it will become.

As America's Relocation Specialist, I have developed an easy to follow Moving Management System that is available for your convenience. The tools in my system will smoothly navigate you step by step down the relocation road. Some useful features are miscellaneous checklists, step-by-step timelines, and filing systems. It's important not to be blindsided because of lack of experience and overlooking key steps or encountering unexpected events.

If you would like to develop your own moving binder, I have listed some tips that have been helpful to my clients.

- Select a colored three-ring binder to hold all your moving paperwork and information. Place tabbed dividers in the binder and label each tab with different moving categories. Some areas to consider would be *Old House*, *Moving Company*, *Moving Checklists and Inventory*, *Banking and Contracts*, *Utilities*, *Purchases and Receipts*, *Travel and Activities*, *Medical and Dental*, *Education*,

Pets, and Vehicles. Adjust the tabs and labels to best fit your needs. Keep a three-hole puncher nearby to punch holes in paperwork as it is accumulated.

- Place a few plastic business card sheets toward the front of your binder. As you accumulate business cards, organize them in these pages. Write notes on each card of store hours, alternative contact numbers, and miscellaneous information regarding these contacts that may be helpful for future reference.
- Continually update a calendar and timeline of events to be placed in this binder. If you would prefer, you may choose to use the calendar feature in your smart phone or laptop computer. Either way, use this calendar as a diary for keeping notes and information as it is accumulated. Don't place the extra burden on yourself by trying to remember everything in your head.
- Include a zip-pouch bag filled with various office supplies including pens, pencils, paperclips, tape, a ministapler, small scissors, and sticky notes.
- Include another zip-pouch bag for receipts.

I tell my clients to find an organizational method that will work best for them and one that they will actually utilize. There is nothing more frustrating than losing an important house-closing document or forgetting a key appointment.

Dump, Donate, or Designate

The time has arrived to get down to business. Hopefully you are a person who likes to clean, declutter, and organize. If this is not your forte, you will need to quickly learn how to become one of those people! You may also consider hiring an expert to assist you or invite a friend to join you and keep you motivated throughout this process.

I tell my clients that the first step is for them to sit down with their calendar and block off uninterrupted time to focus on their house. Ideally, block half or full days. You are up against the clock right now to get your home ready for the market. Make arrangements for your children after school. Have Grandma keep your toddler for the day. Ask your spouse to pick up dinner on his way home from work. Treat this process as if you are working a full-time job. Silence your phone and return calls once you have made some progress. Do whatever you can to allow yourself to stay focused on decluttering your house.

The next step is to schedule a pickup time and date for charity donations as well as additional trash pickup. Set appointments for next week. Go ahead and schedule for two weeks out, too. By setting dates, you will be amazed how motivated and productive you will become to meet the deadlines.

Before you get started, gather empty boxes and heavy-duty trash bags. Wholesale warehouse stores such as Costco, Sam's, or BJ's have plenty of cardboard boxes available upon request. Boxes are great for donations such as glassware. Oversized durable trash bags are good for clothing and linen items.

We all become emotionally attached to our stuff. Somehow we become stuck on holding onto objects and memories from our past. We also fear that we might need these items in the future. The key to the decluttering process is to live in the present and only keep the things that are useful to you today. The following are some questions to ask yourself as you begin this process. Be honest with yourself.

- Why do I have this item?
- Do I have sentimental or emotional reasons for having this item?
- Do I use this item, or is it just something I might use in the future?
- When was the last time I used this item?
- Do I really need this item?
- Am I only keeping this item out of loyalty to a loved one?

Now comes the fun part of beginning the decluttering process. Focus on living in the present. Begin in one room, and don't move to any other rooms until this room is finished. I prefer to start in the kitchen, since I can gain a sense of accomplishment very quickly! Completely empty a cabinet, pantry, closet, or drawer. Once everything is removed, wipe the shelves or drawer. You are now ready to start playing the triple-D game: Dump, Donate, or Designate. As you pick up each item, determine which category the item fits best.

- **Dump.** Throw away items that are broken or outdated, have missing pieces, and are not worthy of donating to a charity. The act of throwing things away is emotionally freeing.
- **Donate.** Place yourself in a "giving" mind-set. Donate the items that you have enjoyed but no longer use or will not have space to store. Let someone enjoy that extra set of glasses or those large purple bath towels. Donate the items that you will no longer be

using, like your snow shovel because you are moving to southern California. Give the gift of clothes to those who can wear them immediately, instead of storing them with the high hopes of losing weight.

- **Designate.** Items in this category will be moved to your next location. Organize these items back into the cabinet, drawer, or closet that you just cleared and cleaned. If the item belongs in another location of the house, go ahead and place it in the correct location. This step will give you a better idea of the amount of items that you will be packing. If you have some items that you just cannot donate at this time, place them in a box labeled "Undecided." Down the road you can donate or designate them.

Decluttering is a therapeutic and cleansing experience that will make you feel emotionally and physically lighter. Once you separate yourself from your stuff, you will find that you don't miss it nearly as much as you thought you would miss it. You will thank yourself for clearing through the majority of your clutter when you are unpacking the boxes at your new home.

An Apple a Day

When athletes prepare to participate in a sporting event, they train many hours. In order to reach their peak performance, athletes will focus on their fitness, nutrition, hydration, recovery, and mental stamina. As strange as it sounds, a move can also feel like running a marathon! It, too, will require you to focus on these same health concepts.

The popular phrase "An apple a day keeps the doctor away" can apply to your life at this very demanding and stressful time. You are now an athlete who has signed up for a championship event. One of the challenges you will encounter is eating healthy. Your time is limited, everything in your kitchen is packed away in a box, and your kids are telling you that they are hungry! The easiest fix is to order a pizza. As much as I love pizza, I can tell you that by the end of your move you will all be very tired of eating pizza! Fast food is another quick solution but will not provide quality fuel necessary for this event.

I instruct my clients to make it a priority to stop at the grocery and stock up on healthy foods and beverages. One of my personal quick-fix favorites is to prepare protein smoothies. I keep my blender handy, purchase some good-flavored high-protein powder, and add in some fresh fruit. I also like to make a quick stop at a Whole Foods salad bar or deli counter to bring home some items to keep in the refrigerator. This is a time to have a friend help you with a meal or call your favorite fresh grill restaurant for a carryout dinner. Do the best that you can during this hectic time. Don't allow yourself to feel guilty that you are unable to prepare a full-course meal for your family.

This is not a good time to start a strict new diet plan or to focus on losing weight. You are already placing enough pressure on yourself. There is no need to feel bad because you cannot stick to a restrictive meal plan. Starvation and hunger pains will only cause your stress level to rise even more. Do the best that you can to maintain your weight, and regroup with your diet goals once your life is back into a normal routine.

Another area that you will need to place some priority on is sleep. Psychological stressors like selling a home can prevent you from getting a good night's sleep. Packing boxes right up until it's time to turn out the lights will make it difficult to drop off into a blissful night's sleep. I am guilty of working nonstop to finish my "to do" list. I know from my own personal experience that lack of sleep causes me to feel irritable, impatient, moody, and unable to concentrate. These traits do not compliment this already stressful situation. Most of all, attempt to get enough sleep so that your immune system does not weaken. No one will benefit from you calling in sick.

Along with adequate rest is the need for exercise. Even in the midst of a nonstop schedule, it is important take a break to attend an exercise class or to take a walk in the park. I have found that Pilates and yoga improve my mood and make me feel relaxed. A clear head makes it so much easier to face your day of nonstop decisions. While the act of moving in itself is good exercise, you do need to be cautious of potential injuries. Be realistic with your personal abilities. Be aware of the weight of the boxes you are packing, and ask for help when moving heavy boxes or objects. The last thing you need is a strained back or injury.

You are the most important moving tool. A good mental break can do wonders for your health, too. Take time to have dinner with your family, go to a movie, or enjoy a good cup of coffee with a friend.

Hiring a Real Estate Agent

Selling your home can be a challenging process. The truth of the matter is that the majority of homeowners need to sell their current home before they can purchase a second home. Therefore, it is key to hire a professional realtor who can ensure you the best possible experience. A confident agent can navigate the real estate system for you while selling your home for top dollar as quickly as possible.

I tell my clients that their first priority is to find a real estate agent. Ideally, locate an agent who is familiar with your neighborhood and most closely fits your personality style. It is important that the realtor you select is a member of the National Association of Realtors, which abides strictly by a code of ethics. To find a realtor, utilize websites such as www.realtor.com or ask your friends, relatives, and coworkers for referrals. With this in mind, to avoid hurt feelings and strained relationships, it is best not to mix friendships with business.

Through your research, select three different real estate agents from three different firms. Make appointments with each of the prospective agents individually, and interview them to find the best agent that will work the hardest for you. In my experience, it is beneficial to hire an agent who has an assistant that can provide additional support if necessary.

Make sure that the realtor you select utilizes a variety of marketing strategies. Through a multiple listing service (MLS), your realtor can place your property on a computerized listing along with other US real estate properties offered for sale. Request that a professional photographer take the photos for your home listing. I have found that there really is a difference in the quality of the photographs, and you want your property to be represented as positively as possible. A good-quality online virtual tour video is important, too. First impressions really do make a difference.

Pricing a home is difficult. As we all learned in economics class, the market is driven by supply and demand. It is understandable that sellers want to make a profit on their real estate investments, but if a home is overpriced, it will lose its "new listing" appeal within the first few weeks of showing. Basically, a property will sell at a price a buyer is willing to pay and a seller is willing to accept. Ask your agent to conduct a comparable market analysis (CMA) to best determine the value of your home. The CMA will give you an informal estimate of your home's value based on comparable sales in your neighborhood. Depending on your time restraints, my suggestion is to price your home to sell. The quicker you have your home under contract, the quicker you can move on to the next step of your relocation process.

It's Show Time

Now that you have found a realtor and are ready to list your home, it's time to transition to selling and marketing mode. You have made an investment in your home, and now you need to put every effort forward to get your greatest return.

Throughout my twenty-five years of working in the corporate world, I benefitted from the opportunity to participate in numerous sales and marketing training courses. Lead sales instructors stress the importance of engaging as many of the five traditionally recognized senses (sight, hearing, taste, smell, and touch) into each promotional message. While it is not feasible to include all five senses in each sales call, I discovered that this concept greatly impacted what a customer would remember about the product you are selling.

In this situation, your house is your product. Your goal is to set your product apart from the competition. A home is not only about square footage, appliances, and paint colors. When looking at your home, your buyers will form impressions through the senses of sight, hearing, taste, smell, and touch. The sight of the freshly planted flowers, the sound of their kids running downstairs on Christmas morning, the taste of the hamburgers grilled in the backyard on the Fourth of July, the smell of pumpkin pie on Thanksgiving, and the touch of sleeping comfortably at night—your buyers want the whole package. Your job is to create an environment that will make your buyers feel like they are home.

The best way to make your buyers feel like your home could be their home is to remove anything that might sidetrack the buyers' senses. I would like to encourage you to review the Dump, Donate, and Designate system that I developed to help you embrace the "less is more" concept. You may want to consider hiring a professional home-staging company to come assist you. It would also be beneficial for you to refer to several resources that are available, including your real estate agent, various decluttering websites, and numerous published materials that focus on successful home-selling strategies.

Over the years, we have sold eight homes all within the first two weeks of going on the market. I am sure that the real estate market had a lot to do with the timing, but I strongly believe that the staging of our homes was a strong factor. The following are some of the selling strategies that I implement when preparing our homes for market.

- Put on your "buyers" glasses, grab a notepad and a pen, and walk around the exterior and interior of you home, considering all the items you are most concerned about when you make a real estate investment. If this is not your specialty, consider having your real estate agent or consultant analyze the situation with you. You have now created your "to do" list. This is where the fun begins!
- Do the best that you can to accommodate your potential buyers' needs. Basically, people want to live in a home that is better than the home where they are living right now! Your buyers' windows may be dirty, but they will expect *your* windows to be clean. Your buyers' bathroom may have bright pink walls, but they will want *your* bathroom walls to be painted in a neutral color. Your buyers' garage may be a total mess, but they will expect *your* garage to fit all their vehicles.
- Paint your front door, and hang a fresh, seasonally appropriate wreath on the door. Pull all the weeds, trim the shrubs, plant new flowers, freshen mulch, and replace the doorknob. Do whatever possible to make the first few steps taken toward your front door as favorable as possible.
- Hire a cleaning company, if possible, to come clean your house weekly. It gets very tiring to keep a home "show ready." Just knowing that the entire house will be cleaned weekly will take some pressure off your schedule at this hectic time. I cannot stress enough the importance of cleanliness. Dirt creates the impression that you really don't care about your property. No one wants to invest in a property that has not been maintained.
- Remove all family and pet photographs from the home. I usually replace the frames hanging on the wall with photographs of pretty scenery of places we have traveled. Your buyers only need to visualize themselves and their life in your home. There is a lot of psychology involved in buying a home.
- If you have pets, hide the fact that you have pets. Attempt to hide bowls, food, toys, or anything that has to do with your animals. I know that this sounds crazy, but this all goes back to the five senses of sight, hearing, smell, taste, and touch. Think about the sight of the backdoor scratches from the dog, the sound of the bird chirping constantly, the smell of the dirty cat-litter box, the touch of the hamster running through the house, or the possible

taste of animal hair in your food! Don't narrow your potential buyer market by assuming that everyone who comes to visit is an animal lover.

Also, take into consideration that many people suffer from pet allergies. On one of our house hunting trips, I can recall looking at a home that had a strong, reeking odor of cat urine. As a whole, we liked the home, but we just couldn't get past the foul smell and the thought of cat hairs floating through the home. Our conversations focused on allergies and the odor more than the qualities of the house. Needless to say, we did not purchase the home.

- Hide or protect the valuables in your home, including prescription drugs and jewelry. Since I don't really own anything of great value, I usually don't get too concerned—although, following one of our recent open houses, I discovered that someone had stolen a pair of my shoes! Who would have thought of shoes? I figure that whoever took my shoes must have really needed them. They probably walked right out of the house wearing my navy loafers!
- Bake brownies! Fill the house with good smells. You know how in the old days when a woman went into labor, the husband was told to go boil water? Well, I believe that it's because the doctor knew it would keep the husband busy while he delivered the baby! A watched pot never boils! The same concept works with baking brownies. For just thirty minutes out of this hectic day, you can get your mind off the pressure of selling your home while creating some awesome smells in your home.
- Dress for success. In business, they say the better you are dressed, the more seriously you will be taken, and this same concept goes for your home. Present your home at the level you want to sell. If you want the higher offer, then you have to show it!
- Confirm that all your bathrooms are clean. I encourage my clients to spray a nice-smelling cleanser in the sinks, wipe and flush each commode, replace empty toilet-paper holders, and place a fresh hand towel along with soap by each sink. Remember, this is your future buyers' potential "dream" home. Who wouldn't dream of using a well-stocked, clean bathroom with a flushed toilet?
- Clean each room in your home and then shut the door. Live within very limited space. Try not to use some of your bathrooms or bedrooms. This time- and energy-saving strategy will

come in handy when a realtor calls on short notice requesting to show your home. When this occurs, straighten the rooms you are living in, open the doors to the closed-off rooms, hide your dirty laundry in the washing machine, turn on the lights, grab the dog, and head out of the house.

- Go out to eat. Keep the kitchen clean. If you do cook, don't cook onions or heavily spiced fried foods, and for sure do not burn the food! Odor may linger in the house. Fully utilize and enjoy the benefit of not being able to cook due to the selling of your home!
- If possible, go out of town! Take a minivacation on a weekend that you know your house has been booked for an open house along with several showings. Not only does this getaway allow you and your family to leave the house ready to show, but it also gives you a break from all the decisions you have been making up to this point.

The Waiting Game

The "For Sale" sign is in the yard, your home is actively on the market, and you are playing the dreaded waiting game. In the majority of these situations, you must sell your current home before you can move forward to your next home. I can recall feeling like my hands were tied. Anxiety can especially rise when your spouse needs to move on to their new job assignment, your kids need to get registered before a new school year begins, and you are continually getting bombarded with questions from people wanting to know the status of your move. Waiting for a home to sell requires a large amount of patience. This might be a good time to refer back to Step 1, when I discussed attitude adjustment!

Ideally, your home sells quickly, and you can move on along with your plans. However, depending on the housing market, sometimes it takes some time and it will be necessary to make alternative plans. In some situations, arrangements can be made that will allow your family to live in temporary housing until your home sells. In other situations, the family may be required to temporarily divide, while the spouse goes on to his or her new job assignment and the remaining family members stay behind until housing details are finalized. Remember Step 1, when I discussed a flexible attitude? I tell my clients that flexibility is key.

There are several issues that can arise that can complicate the timing of events. One common issue is getting your children registered in school before the school year or midsemester begins. If your children will be attending public schools, most of the time you will need to establish residency at your new location to show that you are living within the school zone limits. Another dilemma is if you are a two-career family and both spouses are committed to deadlines surrounding their start dates. A third possible situation is that you are five months pregnant, you cannot travel in your final trimester, and your home hasn't sold yet. The fact of the matter is that there are a lot of issues that will be beyond your control.

One step that you can take at this point, whether you have sold your home or not, is to spend some time researching housing options in your new city. I have found that the best way to gather information is by locating a real estate agent who is highly familiar with the area that you are moving to. In Step 1 of this book, I reviewed some points to consider when hiring a real estate agent. The same advice applies in this situation, except you will be taking a shot in the dark.

It can be risky to select an unknown real estate agent in an unfamiliar market, especially when you are moving long distance. I have found that a lot of this selection process is based on your gut instinct. You need to find an agent who is enthusiastic, quickly returns your calls, gives you confidence and encouragement, and provides current housing research materials. You deserve someone who makes you a priority and appears to be working for only you even though he or she may have several clients. Since you may be hiring an agent sight unseen, it will be of utmost importance to hire someone with strong credentials. The person you hire will be your eyes, ears, and expert from many miles away.

One option in finding a realtor in your new city is to ask your current real estate agent for a referral. Real estate companies have the ability to search top-ranked real estate agents throughout the country. A second option is to get a referral from someone you may already know that lives in your future location. Our tax accountant, who just so happened to live in Georgia, was able to give us a referral for a real estate agent prior to our move to Atlanta. Sometimes your employer will have a recommendation list of real estate agents that work their employee relocations. Another option is to research potential real estate agents online. There are sites such as www.realestateagent.com and www.realtor.com, or you can go directly to a broker website and contact one of their lead agents.

One final note—sometimes you don't select the real estate agent that can best fit your buying needs. We have had this happen on various occasions. It is important to remember that in this particular relationship, you may discover that after spending some face-to-face time, your personalities and purchasing styles just don't "click." While this is a tough predicament, it is important that you feel well represented by someone who truly understands your housing needs.

Step 3

Where Should You Live?

House Hunting

Let's assume that all your hard work has paid off and you have sold your home. Now it's time to find a new home. Just like every other aspect of this move, this step will involve emotion. It will be important to stay focused, rational, and business minded as you make this high-value investment.

I inform my clients that their first consideration is to determine their housing budget. The best approach is to avoid looking at homes outside of your resources and target the homes that are priced within your allowance. With this said, be prepared to raise your budget if necessary. I have found that we always hope to stick to our original estimates but usually find it necessary to increase our funds.

Once you have determined the price range of the home you would like to purchase, it will be necessary to obtain a mortgage preapproval letter from a bank or mortgage company that is based locally within the area you are purchasing the home. Your real estate agent can provide you with recommendations.

The second consideration is to write down everything you want in a home. List your top five "must-haves." Your goal is to target your must-haves even though your list may include several items that would be "nice to have." Once you have determined your budget, have obtained a mortgage preapproval letter, and have set your must-haves, your realtor can narrow the community and housing search criteria for your new home and provide you with periodic MLS selections and new-listings alerts. You can also research homes online at sites such as www.realtor.com, www.trulia.com, or www.zillow.com.

The third consideration is to research various communities. Your realtor can provide you information regarding areas of cities you should consider. The following are some items that we consider when selecting a community.

- **School district.** It has been shown that homes in higher-ranked school districts appreciate faster than those in lower-ranked school districts. This is also a consideration if your children will be attending public schools.
- **Commute to work.** Determine how long it will take you to drive to and from work. Determine rush-hour patterns and various traffic conditions. You may also need to consider the circumstances of your commute to drop your children at daycare or school prior to driving to work.
- **Community demographics.** Does the average age, education level, and lifestyle of the population that lives in the community match your needs?
- **Community institutions.** Are you satisfied with the shopping, restaurants, places of worship, and entertainment options in the community?
- **Homeowners association (HOA).** These associations can protect the value of homes in the community, but they can also have strict neighborhood rules and annual dues. How much will you need to pay annually, and will this fee fit into your budget?
- **Activity level.** Are there big flood lights that come on in the parking lot behind the neighborhood that will shine into your bedroom at night? Can you make a left turn out of the neighborhood during rush hour in the morning? It's important to preview the community during the daytime and nighttime as well as on weekdays and weekends.
- **Safety.** Will you feel safe? What are the crime rates?

The fourth consideration is the actual house-hunting search. In my experience, I have found it helpful to have my children tour a few schools in our targeted communities prior to selecting a home. It's the little things they notice like the school mascot, the location of the lockers, or the size of the football stadium that may resonate with them. We usually base our home selection on the schools that our children like the most. When planning your house-hunting trip, you will want to keep school tours in mind. Call the schools ahead of time to set tour appointments, and confirm that the schools will be in session on the days of your visit. If you will be requiring day care or preschool for younger children, this would be a good time to make those preview appointments, too.

Over the years, I have discovered some helpful hints to help us stay organized while looking at houses. There have been times that we have viewed more than fifteen homes in a day or even fifty homes on one trip, and it is easy to become quite confused and disoriented. There is so much information to absorb in a short period of time. The following are some pointers that I encourage my clients to apply to help them stay organized while evaluating their options.

- **Moving Management System.** I have created this binder to provide guidance throughout your move. Organization is key, and I have furnished some tools such as checklists, calendars, and filing systems that can enhance your productivity.
- **Map of the city.** I can recall arriving in Los Angeles, Atlanta, Milwaukee, and Nashville feeling totally disoriented. Finding a single home among millions of homes is quite overwhelming. A map is invaluable when driving hundreds of miles around a city. I found that I felt more logistically solid when I marked the map with areas of homes, schools, and communities that we had previewed.
- **Food and drink.** Once you start the day house hunting, you will be placed on a tight schedule of appointments. We have encountered several times when we have skipped lunch and have hardly had time to stop for a drink. Before heading out with the realtor, make sure you all have a big bottle of water and some snacks or protein bars. There is nothing worse than being hungry or thirsty and not having time to stop. Concentration will be key.
- **Investor role.** Over the years, we have sold each of our eight homes in less than two weeks. All our homes have sold within asking price, with several selling above asking price. I truly believe that our real estate investment success has been based on the fact that we purchase each home with our future buyers in mind. While our realtors may get frustrated with our critical eye, we feel it is necessary for the sake of our investment.
- **Inspector role.** When viewing homes, pretend like you are the inspector rather than the potential buyer. Don't ignore the red flags that you see. If a steep driveway, water retention pond, poor

curb appeal, or damp basement makes you feel uneasy, most likely these items will disturb your future buyers, too. Some issues cannot be changed, and the items that can be changed may be too expensive to correct.

Request to see the disclosure statements of homes that you are considering to purchase. A seller must disclose personal knowledge of problems that could affect the property's value or desirability. We have avoided making some bad investment decisions by reviewing the disclosure information prior to us placing an offer on a home. We have escaped homes with documented termites, mold in walls, a history of flooded basements, and major structural issues, which were all disclosed in the statements. Trust your instincts.

I tell my clients that regardless of the age of the home, they should *always* hire a reputable outside inspector that can provide an objective, comprehensive analysis of the home's major systems and components, both honestly and objectively, apart from anyone's interests other than the future owners. This step protects your interests and your future investment. It is important that the seller provide you a one-year home warranty to cover the major systems in the home, such as HVAC (heating, ventilation, and air conditioning), water heater, dishwasher, and pool pumps.

One last item to consider is to have your realtor contact the local authority planning department to see if there are any planning applications within the chosen zip code. This information will provide you with potential developments that might be built near the homes you are researching. We were seriously considering putting an offer on a home until we discovered it was going to have a middle school built directly behind it. This would not have been that big of an issue to us personally, but it could have killed some future deals when we went to sell the home.

- **Nickname homes.** After a full day of house hunting, I have found it difficult to remember details about each property. To keep things simple, we started giving each house that we reviewed our own personal nickname. We found it much easier to recall details about properties based on the nicknames.

  The "shampoo house" was a home that we viewed that had at least fifty shampoo bottles on the master-bathroom counter. We named another home the "cat house" because it had several cats roaming around during our visit. One of our funnier names was the "potty house." As we walked by a bathroom that had its door open, we came upon the homeowner sitting on the toilet! We had no problem remembering the "potty house" listing!

- **Check your mobile phone signal.** While walking through homes, I encourage my clients to turn on their mobile phones and check the strength of the service signal within the house. Avoid getting a home with communications black spots. This is something that the majority of people do not consider. I have friends who cannot talk on their mobile phones from within their homes due to lack of service. Keep in mind that you may need to change mobile phone service or just not have good-quality access to mobile phone service.
- **Take pictures.** With the homeowners' permission, I like to take pictures as a form of documentation for those homes that we would like to revisit. Ideally, they will have professionally taken photos on their website and brochures. Pictures are a good way to refresh your memory of home details.
- **Check if a handyman is needed.** If you are not a handyman or you don't have free qualified manpower available, I would suggest that you not purchase a fixer-upper if you are trying to stay within a designated budget. Repairs and upgrades always cost more money and time than you expect.

  With this said, I understand that the majority of homes will need some repairs and upgrades. We have encountered this situation several different times. Prior to purchasing these homes, we contacted a contractor to come give us a rough cost estimate for the necessary upgrades. This gave us additional information to consider when placing an offer on these properties. Our home inspection prior to purchasing the home also provided us a clearer picture of items that may need to be replaced or repaired. Regardless, confirm that the seller will be providing a home warranty with the purchase of the home.
- **Ask for the realtor's advice.** I always ask my realtor, "If I called you tomorrow and told you that I needed to sell my home ASAP, which one of the properties that we viewed would you feel most confident selling? Which home do you feel would sell the fastest? Which home is located in the best-selling location?" These questions will allow you to receive objective feedback from your realtor.

After many full days of house hunting, stress, and some emotional meltdowns, you are bound to feel the heaviness of this difficult decision. The goal is to find a house and start getting your life back to some normalcy. Just remember that all your efforts will be well worth it finding the next house that you will call "Home Sweet Home."

Deal or No Deal

You have spent the last several days or weeks looking at homes. This might be a good time to refer back to Step 1, where I discussed decision making and listing pros and cons to help you determine which home will best fit your needs. This is also a good time to trust your gut feelings. Are you ready to make a home offer? It is our preference to sleep on our decision at least one night or even wait a couple weeks—though we have placed an offer on a home after spending just fifteen minutes in it. You will need to evaluate the market. It can be heartbreaking if someone else beats you to the punch and acquires your dream home.

I tell my clients that if they would like to place an offer on a home, they should examine comparable sales and market conditions with their realtor. The last thing you want is to get into a situation where you offer more than the home will appraise. In a competitive market, it is easy to get pulled into a bidding war. We have been placed in this situation numerous times. It can feel quite stressful to get emotionally attached to a home and fear that someone else will win the battle. This is a situation where you need to stay focused and not allow your attachments to override your finances! Stay calm, cool, and collected. The best house listing, within your price range, may hit the market tomorrow.

The famous real estate guru Warren Buffet once quoted, "You ought to be able to explain why you're taking the job you're taking, why you're making the investment you're making, or whatever it may be. And if it can't stand applying pencil to paper, you'd better think it through some more. And if you can't write an intelligent answer to those questions, don't do it." What he was basically saying is that every deal must work on paper before it will ever be able to work in real life. The same will hold true with making a real estate decision.

If you haven't found a home at this time, don't get desperate or feel pressured to act on what you have seen. While it is very discouraging and concerning, you can wait and make another house hunting trip when new properties come on the market. I know that this is not at all convenient, but it is very necessary to stay true to making the best decision. I flew more than two thousand miles between Los Angeles, California, and Atlanta, Georgia, four times in six weeks in order to achieve the best real estate investment. Stay true to your goal.

Over the years, we have been lucky to work with some of the most professional and knowledgeable real estate representatives. With this said, you need to remember that realtors work for a paycheck. They earn a living by selling and buying homes. While it is nice to build a friendship with your realtor, I have found that the majority of the time, we never see our realtor again once the house has closed and the contracts are signed. It really comes down to money and the time that they can devote to a client in order to earn their salary. I can't help but think of the 2007 movie *Jerry Maguire*: "Show me the money!"

The reason I am bringing this up is because after about two to three days of house hunting, we have had times that our realtor has started to pressure us about committing to contract. We have had situations in which our realtor pushed us to buy a home with mold or termites or even structural issues. The truth of the matter is that we, too, want to commit, but if the house is not right, it is not right! Earlier in this step, I mentioned that there are times that you will need change realtors because they are not representing your best interests. I know from personal experience that while you do lose some valuable time rehiring an agent, you will be happier getting an agent who can patiently wait to find the home that best fits your needs. I tell my clients that this is a big investment that they will own long after the realtor has gone.

Temporary Housing

In between the selling of one home and the purchase of another, you may require temporary housing. Adding this step to your move can be somewhat of a nuisance, but sometimes it's your only option. This extra step may cost you additional moving expenses, so your moving budget may determine the type of temporary housing that you acquire.

Determine how long you will require temporary housing. Will you need housing for a few weeks or for a full year? Do you want to rent furniture, provide your own furniture, or rent a fully furnished property? Will you require storage space? Do you need a pet-friendly rental?

You have several options for short-term housing. You can rent an apartment or home, make long-term reservations at an extended-stay motel, or even live temporarily with family or friends. Your real estate agent can provide you rental listings, or you can research options online through websites such as www.corporatehousing.com, www.apartmentguide.com, or www.google.com. If your move is work related, your human resources department may be able to provide you assistance.

The following are some items to consider when selecting short-term living.

- square-footage requirements
- full kitchen
- lease commitments, rates, discounts, and deposits
- proximity to your new community, schools, and work
- Wi-Fi service
- post office mailbox
- washer and dryer
- covered parking
- storage space
- pet-friendliness

If you decide to rent an apartment or home that is not already furnished, you will need to determine how you would like to furnish the property and how much you want to spend. Rental companies such as Rent-A-Center can provide everything including home decor, electronics, appliances, housewares, and bedroom essentials. You can rent items by the week or longer, and all items will be delivered and set up.

The other option is to have your personal home goods delivered to your short-term property. The best part about this option is that you can sleep in your own bed! The worst part about this option is that you will acquire additional moving expenses, since your belongings will be moved twice. If the property you rent is not large enough for all your belongings, you may need to place the majority of your goods into storage and have a portion of your things delivered to your short-term housing.

I inform my clients that if they should decide to do a partial delivery, they should be prepared to do some preplanning prior to packing all their belongings. I have found that placing everything that you would like to move to temporary housing in one room helps keep items separated so that boxes can be marked appropriately. I will be discussing this process in more detail in Step 4.

After years of experiencing "temporary living," we have determined that it is easiest to reside at an extended-stay motel. While the living conditions are not as comfortable as a home, the setup for the money can offer several advantages.

- fully furnished (with televisions already connected to cable!)
- fully equipped kitchen with refrigerator, stove top, and microwave
- daily cleaning service
- bedding and towels laundered daily
- free Wi-Fi
- no need to set up and cancel utilities (this can be a real pain!)
- discounted rates (stay more and save more) and no lease requirements
- daily breakfast provided
- on-site guest laundry (request a room near the laundry room)
- business center with printer access
- pet-friendliness (request a lower-level room)
- the feeling of having a little "vacation" after a hectic move
- swimming pool, fitness room, and outdoor grills
- no need to set up a residence move-in and move-out step

Just remember at this point of your move that you are doing the best you can do given the circumstances you have been handed. Continue to look forward and feel good about everything that has been accomplished. As Zig Ziglar would say, "Be firm on principle but flexible on method!"

Hiring a Moving Company

You will need to decide the best way to move all your belongings to your new home. You can hire a moving company to complete this entire process or simply rent a truck and do it yourself. It all comes down to your budget, time, distance, manpower, and the square footage of the home to which you are moving. A corporate move with a job transfer typically provides you a relocation budget that includes packing and transportation of your belongings. You will need to check with the human resource department at your company to determine what is covered under their moving policies.

Another option is the POD System, in which an empty storage container is delivered directly to your home. This option gives you the flexibility of packing your belongings at your own pace while loading them into the POD unit. Once you are ready to move, PODS will pick up your container and drive it across town or across the country. This company can also provide secure short-term and long-term storage if necessary.

I inform my clients that the best way for them to start the evaluation process for hiring a team is to get quotes from three different moving companies. After scheduling appointments, a sales representative from each company will come to your home and assess all your belongings. Make sure that you tell each company the same items that are being moved so that the prices can be evenly compared.

It is important to evaluate and research various moving companies online. You can also inquire with your family, friends, and coworkers about their moving experiences with various companies. Typically, a long-distance mover is affiliated with a Van Lines or carrier that covers the entire United States. These companies file under the US Department of Transportation's Federal Motor Carrier Safety Administration (FMCSA). Confirm that the company you have selected is registered with the Department of Transportation. You may also consider research websites such as MovingScam.com. This type of website will post articles and message boards where individuals can comment on moving company problems.

Confirm that the moving company that you select provides good insurance. It can feel quite unsettling to realize that everything you own is balanced on eighteen wheels at the mercy of one driver. The goal is for the move to go smoothly, but accidents can happen, and some of your items could be lost or damaged during shipment. Under federal law, interstate movers must offer two different liability options. Full value protection requires your mover to be responsible for the replacement value of lost or damaged goods for your entire shipment. Released value protection requires the mover to assume liability for no more than $0.60 per pound per article. I would suggest that you discuss these two options with your moving representative. Full value protection is more expensive than released value protection. Even though a full value protection plan is more expensive, we always choose this option for the added peace of mind.

Moving companies can provide a variety of services. They can be hired to pack your belongings, custom build crates for extremely fragile items, provide all packing materials, transport your home goods as well as your vehicles, provide short-term and long-term storage, and unpack and arrange your belongings. You will need to determine the magnitude of the services required prior to a company representative arriving to determine an estimated cost.

Once the moving company agent arrives, make sure that he or she pays attention to the details and is shown every single item that you plan to move. Don't forget to show the estimator everything in the attic, basement, garage, as well as items you have stored off site. Get a quote in writing and read the small print. Do not sign anything until you fully understand the terms and conditions. Beware of lowball offers. As the saying goes, "You get what you pay for." This is also a good time to discuss the availability of dates for packing, loading, transporting, and unloading your possessions.

One final note is to discuss with your agent any items that will require special attention. This might include items such as a valuable piano, wine collection, antique car, or billiard table. Your personal vehicles can also be transported from door to door. We have transported vehicles in our moving truck as well as independently. It all comes down to cost, space, and preference. I would suggest paying a little extra to have your vehicle covered or protected against highway debris.

Moving with Pets

Your pets are an important part of the family. I know that our golden retrievers are our most valued possessions! The better you plan, the more smoothly your pets can transition to your new home. Keeping their discomfort and stress to a minimum is essential.

I inform my clients that prior to moving their pets, they should take them to their vet to have shots updated and to acquire copies of current vet records and vaccination certificates. Inform the vet of your move so that he or she can anticipate vaccinations or medications that may be required in your new state. You may also consider the kennel cough vaccine or other vaccines that will be necessary for travel or boarding. Consider getting your pet's prescriptions refilled, and request a sedative if your pet gets anxious traveling long distances in a car. Typically, as a safety precaution, sedatives are not prescribed for a pet that is flying. It is important that animals stay alert and are able to brace themselves during turbulence or similar traveling conditions. One final consideration is to update your pet's microchip information. Since your contact information will be changing, the correct contact information needs to be on file in case your pet should get lost.

I have found it helpful to schedule boarding for your pet the day before the packers and moving truck arrives. This is a confusing time for everyone, and the last thing you want is for your pet to escape. I also request that our dogs be bathed and groomed prior to picking them up from the kennel. It sure makes a long-distance drive a lot nicer when your pets smell clean and their nails are trimmed.

When planning your travel arrangements, research hotels to ensure that they are pet friendly. It is best to speak with someone directly at the hotel, since online pet policies may not be updated. We lived for almost three months in a Marriott Residence Inn with our golden retriever. We were required to pay an extra pet deposit, but overall the experience was positive. For added convenience, request a room that is located on the ground level, ideally with a walkout patio. We placed a "Do Not Disturb" sign on our doorway to ensure that housekeeping did not accidentally let our dog out. We didn't want to be singing the song, "Who let the dogs out, who, who, who, who?" As a kind gesture, we also tipped our room attendant frequently, considering we were housing a rather large dog.

Pets are typically transported by car or airline. Determining the best route of travel will depend on the distance you are traveling, the type of pet you own, and the size of your pet. We have made many moves by car with our dogs. The most difficult part of this, between all the boxes and suitcases, is to leave enough room in the vehicle for the pet! A more expensive and logistically challenging route of pet transportation is by air.

One option is to bring your pet on your US domestic flight. Pets can fly with you if they are small enough to fit comfortably in a kennel under the seat directly in front of you. Airlines limit the number of pets per flight, so it is important for you to contact the airlines early, since pets are accepted on a first-come, first-serve basis.

Since our golden retrievers were too big to fit under the seat in front of us, we decided to have the experts make all the necessary arrangements for their transportation. Pet relocation services professionally move all sorts of pets, including dogs, cats, horses, donkeys, exotic birds, or even frogs. These specialized services stay abreast of up-to-date travel requirements and documents required for animal transportation. Even though this route is expensive, we have gained a great deal of peace of mind knowing that every detail is covered.

I inform my clients that the best way to locate a reputable pet transport company is through a referral from their moving company or through online research. The following are some items to consider when selecting a pet relocation service.

- Does the service provide a customized flight schedule for your pet on a pet-friendly, climate-controlled airline with 24/7 flight tracking? Do they keep you updated on flight numbers, departure and arrival airports, and pertinent contact information? It's nice to have the ability to track your pet's journey. We also appreciated the special attention that was given to our twelve-year-old golden retriever, which suffered from severe arthritis, and our young golden retriever puppy, which needed some extra loving.
- Does the service consult directly with your pet's veterinarian to ensure that all vaccine and health history is updated and required paperwork is complete?
- Does the service arrange drivers on both ends for both pre- and postboarding if necessary? Our service picked up our dogs from our home, delivered them to a prearranged airport kennel for the night, and boarded them on their flight the following morning. The service also completed postflight arrangements and delivered our two dogs to a prearranged kennel of our choice to stay until we arrived and settled in our home. A good time to research potential kennels is during your house-hunting trip.

The best part about a pet relocation service is that they will take care of everything from the time they pick up your pet until they deliver your pet to your new home. The worst part about a pet relocation service is the expense. Pricing will vary among services depending on the services that you would like to have provided. Typically, a pet relocation can start off at a minimum of $1,000 for complete door-to-door service in all US cities and states. In your pricing, you will also need to include the cost of a hard exterior travel crate that meets airline standards. I encourage my clients to purchase their travel crate directly from the pet service they hire to ensure that airline guidelines are met.

Step 4

Saying Your Good-Byes

Mail, Utilities, and Memberships

In order for the postal service to forward your mail from your old address to your new address, you will need to complete change-of-address forms on the US Postal Service website www.changeofaddress.org. On this site, you will have the option of entering the date that you would like to start forwarding your mail, along with important contact information. I recommend that my clients obtain a PO box number through their local postal service while they are living at a temporary address such as a motel. Make sure to print a copy of your change-of-address request form and place it in your moving management binder for future reference.

I inform my clients that this is also a good time to update their address with their bank and investment accounts, credit cards, mobile phones, schools, businesses, magazine subscriptions, vehicle loans, along with family and friends. To avoid missing any important billing statements or deadlines during this transition period, I personally prefer to make payments online or set up automatic payments. One other step to consider is to request that the new owners of your home mail you any personal items that are received within the first couple months after closing. I do this by leaving a couple preaddressed USPS flat-rate boxes with the new owners.

Once you have established a moving date, contact your utility companies to discontinue your service. Meter readings need to be taken on the day of closing so that all services after that date will be the responsibility of the new owner. Make a list of each company, telephone number, date, and person that you talked with regarding the discontinuation of service. Some services to consider are gas and electric, water, telephone, Internet, cable or satellite television, and trash removal. Keep this list updated and placed in your moving management binder for easy access if questions should arise.

Depending on the commitments that you have made with various memberships, it may be necessary to send a written request to discontinue your contracts. Some fitness facilities require a thirty-day notice prior to stopping your membership. Some golf and tennis clubs may require two years or more of membership dues to meet cancellation requirements. We have been burned with contract commitments that exceed the amount of time that we have actually lived in the city. I encourage my clients to thoroughly review entire contracts, honing in on the fine print, prior to committing to any kind of membership.

Packing the House

People cringe at the thought of packing everything that they own into a cardboard box. Packing can be physically demanding. Whether you are packing yourself or hiring a moving company, the process involves a lot of time, trash, trucks, and even turbulence!

Back in Step 2, I encouraged you to take the "less is more" concept and Dump, Donate, or Designate all your stuff. This is the point where you don't want to pack anything that you don't want to unpack. As you are working, it might be helpful to sing along with the theme song from the Disney movie *Frozen*, "Let It Go!"

I always inform my clients that packing the house is the calm before the storm! My goal is to get you organized before the movers or your helpers arrive. If you have hired packers, the minute they hit your doorway, they will officially be on the clock, and your house will quickly turn into a fury of paper and boxes. It will be too late at this point for you to get organized.

Documentation

Before you start packing and disassembling your home, I would suggest that you grab your camera and take photographs of everything in your home, including the items in your cabinets, drawers, and closets. These snapshots will provide excellent documentation for potential insurance claims and also provide some excellent evidence of every item that was packed. I know from my own personal experience that it can feel very disturbing to observe a large semitruck pull away from your home with everything that you own sitting on only eighteen wheels!

Photographs can also provide you a great memory and planning tool. My clients have also found it helpful to take snapshots of the wiring on the back of televisions or anything that requires assembly. You can refer back to these photographs down the road when you are putting everything back together. Photographs are also a good visual resource to utilize when determining the placement of furniture, rugs, and decor in your interior design space.

Children and Pets

This is the time to call on your family or friends to assist you with your young children. In the mix of the clutter and chaos, you need to stay focused on the packing and not get sidetracked by being a caregiver. This can also be a stressful time for your pets, too. Finding alternative housing or daycare, such as a kennel or even a neighbor's fenced yard, will be helpful.

Keep Track of Your Stuff

Moving is the easiest time to misplace your keys, wallet, mobile phone, and important paperwork. In this state of turmoil, we have misplaced these items, and it is no fun to spend time hunting through already packed boxes or very full trashcans to locate them. I suggest that my clients solve this potential problem by designating an empty drawer or container as their "important stuff" location. I tell my clients that they might even want to place a "Do Not Disturb" sign at this location!

Some other items to place in your "important stuff" location are all additional house keys, garage-door openers, appliance manuals, and home instructions. Your buyers will need to obtain these at your house closing.

Family Suitcases

Every member of the family should pack a suitcase that includes everything that he or she will need for a few days. Since everything you own will be packed away in boxes, remember to pack key items such as reading glasses, prescription medications, and telephone chargers. Prior to the packers arriving, place the suitcases in your car, ready to take to your accommodations for the night. I highly advise staying at a motel or with a loved one during the next few days of packing and moving out of your home. It is so much easier to retreat to a calm, established surrounding verses living in a house full of boxes.

Temporary Housing Boxes

If you will be moving into temporary living accommodations prior to your permanent home, now is the best time for you to set aside and prepack the items that will be needed during this transitional period. I encourage my clients to look at their calendar and attempt to preplan for upcoming events. Sometimes it is better to overpack than to underpack. House closing dates can get delayed, and sometimes it is necessary to extend temporary living timeframes.

Besides all the typical housing items, such as bedding and kitchen supplies, I have listed some additional items that I have my clients consider for their temporary living boxes. Keep in mind that it is extremely difficult, if not impossible, to retrieve items once they go into storage. Therefore, anticipate upcoming events such as weddings, holidays, and vacations that will require special attire. As you prepare these boxes, place them in an isolated room or an area labeled "Temporary Housing."

- clothing for current season and possible transition season (winter coat)
- school supplies, paperwork, backpacks, gym clothes, and instruments
- medical records, prescription drugs, and devices (sleep apnea machine!)
- dress attire for a job interview, wedding, or unforeseen funeral
- vacation items (swim suits, golf clubs, tennis racquets, ski equipment)
- holiday decorations or gifts for various celebrations (weddings, birthdays)
- important document file (passports, birth certificates, marriage license)
- annual tax documents and receipts
- children's toys (video game system, games, toys, chargers, batteries)
- pet medications, vaccine and medical records, leashes, and toys
- extra set of car keys and safety deposit box keys
- vacuum, mop, and broom
- tool box

First Night Survival Boxes

I warn my clients that the day they move into their new home will be very exhausting. Every room will be loaded with boxes that will all look the same. To make things easier, in big red lettering, label each box that contains the items that you will need your first night or two. The following are some items that I recommend my clients consider for their survival boxes.

- bedding, pillows, clock, flashlight, pajamas
- towels, soap, shampoo, toilet paper, shower curtain and rings
- temporary window coverings
- first-aid kit (ibuprofen, Band-Aids, antiseptic)
- box cutters, scissors, tape, notepad, pen
- telephone
- DVD player, new movies, activities for kids, video game system
- kitchen survival items, paper products (coffee pot, paper goods, utensils)
- extension cord, three-way plug

Snack Box

Clean through your kitchen cabinets and pull out food or snack items that can be placed into your family snack box. This can include cereal, crackers, peanut butter, granola bars, pretzels, or any items that can easily be accessed by your family. It's also good to have plenty of bottled water and paper products available, too. The worst thing is to be hungry when packing, unpacking, and moving.

Portable Office Box

I tell my clients that one of the best ways for them to stay organized in the middle of transition is to create a portable office box. In this box, keep items that you would normally access at your desk at home. This is a good place to keep the moving binder that you created or the Moving Management System that I developed. Some other items to consider are notepads, pens, tape, sticky notes, scissors, paper clips, staplers, envelopes, and stamps. This box is a good place to store receipts, order forms, moving company information, house closing forms, and all other documentation that you may need to have easy access to.

Cleaning Supply Box

Moving companies are not permitted to place aerosol or liquid cleaning products on their trucks. Therefore, designate a cleaning product box to place all these supplies. It is helpful to have access to this box when cleaning your home for your future homeowners. I have found that friends and neighbors are always eager to accept cleaning supply donations.

Tool Box

A portable toolbox is key when moving. Some tools that you may frequently utilize could include a cordless drill, claw hammer, measuring tape, torpedo level, crescent wrench, pliers, screw driver, socket set, assortment of nails, dry wall anchors, and picture hanging kits. Several box cutters, distributed throughout various rooms in the house, are quite useful when unpacking boxes.

Miscellaneous Parts Box

One of the worst things that can happen when you arrive to your new home is to not be able to locate the screws, bolts, and hardware necessary to reassemble your bed or furniture. It's like looking for a needle in a haystack, if your furniture pieces and hardware get lost.

To solve this issue, I recommend that my clients create an organized location to keep track of the miscellaneous parts. Place all the small, loose pieces into well-labeled Ziploc bags for each piece of furniture. Then place all these Ziploc bags into your miscellaneous parts box. You could even use a bright-red felt-tip marker to label this box so that it stands apart from your other boxes.

Everything Else Boxes

If you are packing yourself, start with the items that are used least frequently. The sooner you can get started, the less pressure you will experience as you get closer to your actual moving date. The following are some packing suggestions that I have found helpful over the years.

- Purchase a clipboard with lined paper and keep inventory by labeling each box with an inventory number, room, and item description.
- Order wholesale-priced boxes in bulk online and have them delivered directly to your door. Hardware stores such as Lowes or Home Depot also have competitively priced boxes and moving

supplies, but you will need to have a rather large vehicle to transport them home.

- Remember that same-size boxes stack the best. Use smaller boxes for heavier items such as books, toys, and picture frames. Place heavier items at bottom of a box and place lighter items toward the top.
- Quality packing materials such as bubble wrap and moving paper are useful, but clothing items and towels are also effective for cushioning fragile items. Socks can be used for protecting individual glassware. Styrofoam plates can be placed between glass dishes to prevent them from breaking.
- You can never purchase too much heavy packing tape and labeling markers!
- Host a "packing party." Ladies can handle the kitchen glassware, and men can tackle the garage hardware.
- If for some reason the items you are packing are not in the correct room, take those items to the correct location so that they will be labeled and packed appropriately. Upon arrival at your new destination, you will appreciate the fact that items were delivered and unpacked in the correct location.

A Sense of Humor

If you really look at your life as a whole, isn't it just amusing? I have found throughout my life that having a sense of humor has allowed me to face some difficult circumstances. In fact, studies have shown that humor appears to be an important part of stress relief and human survival.

I wanted to mention the importance of maintaining a sense of humor at this time because I understand the uncertainties that a relocation can bring. At times, moving can feel like a complete fiasco. Your best-laid plans can go haywire at any moment, leaving you in a totally different situation. I tell my clients that throughout their move, they need to allow themselves to see the lighter side of their absurdities and laugh—otherwise all they will want to do is cry!

My father gave me the gift of having a sense of humor. He had a way of being able to make light of what could be a very dark situation. Growing up in a family of six, in a very small house, required a lot of humor! The famous comedian Betty White once said, "It's your outlook on life that counts. If you take yourself too lightly and don't take yourself too seriously, pretty soon you can find humor in our everyday lives. And sometimes it can be a lifesaver."

Move-Out Day

The boxes are packed, and your bills are paid, and the time has come for move-out day! I tell my clients that their main assignment for this day is to be available to answer numerous questions from their moving team. If for some reason you cannot be home on move-out day, it will be important to have someone represent you. This day can potentially be a "Murphy's Law Day" in which anything that can go wrong will go wrong! This might be a good time to review Step 1 of this book, in which I encouraged you to focus on having a positive attitude. The power of positive thinking doesn't mean that you keep your head in the sand and ignore all the difficulties of this relocation. Positive thinking and self-talk will allow you to think that the best is going to happen, not the worst.

Moving out of your home can stir up a wide range of emotions. You have created a lot of memories within these walls, and now you are getting ready to hand the keys to someone else. Before leaving each of our homes, I follow a sentimental routine in which I walk from one empty room to the next empty room and sit quietly, recalling memories. I intentionally try to remember the numerous happy times as well as sad times—good times as well as bad times. I say silent prayers of thanks for what we were given within the walls of our home and prayers for future happiness for those who will reside in our home once we are gone.

Miranda Lambert, a well-known country music singer, released a hit in 2010 called "The House That Built Me." Her words are so real as she describes going back to the home where she spent many years of her childhood. I like the verse, "If I could just come in, I swear I'll leave. Won't take nothing but a memory from the house that built me." I feel that every home that I have lived in has built me, too. The memories that are built in a home can be powerful, and leaving those surroundings to walk into the unknown requires me to have blind faith. Charles Stanley once said, "Oftentimes God demonstrates His faithfulness in adversity by providing for us what we need to survive. He does not change our painful circumstances. He sustains us through them."

The weather can be another area of concern on moving day. Thinking back over our relocations, we have moved in all types of weather conditions. I can recall a snowy winter moving day in Milwaukee, Wisconsin, when I wore my winter coat and gloves all day because every door in the house was open. Our oldest son, Adam, who was just one month old at the time, was asleep bundled in his bassinet in a small bathroom that just so happened to be the only warm room in our house. I can also recall another moving day in the heat of the summer in Nashville, Tennessee, when we all felt like we lost ten pounds in sweat! Regardless of the situation, I encourage my clients to try to maintain a flexible, "go with the flow" attitude. Just like a boy scout, always be prepared for whatever may come your way.

On move-out day, the moving crew typically arrives first thing in the morning with a very large semitruck. Since the truck may block your entire driveway and possibly even some of the street, you will need to park your vehicles down the street prior to their arrival. You may also want to give your neighbors a warning in case they too will need to move their vehicles. Once the loading process begins, the semitruck will not leave its spot until everything has been loaded from your home.

I tell my clients that a happy crew is a productive crew. As a courtesy, provide your moving team with cold water, snacks, and lunch. Keep in mind that your movers are doing very hard physical work and need to keep fueled and hydrated. I have found that bringing in pizza, hamburgers, or sandwiches are good meal alternatives for feeding a large crew. I have also found that it is important to keep lots of toilet paper on hand, too, if you know what I mean!

Once the house is totally empty, you will discover the dust and dirt that has been accumulating under all your furniture. I feel that it is a nice gesture to leave your home clean and fresh for your new homeowners. Over the years, we have cleaned our homes ourselves, but my preference is to hire a cleaning service. After many tiring days, it's nice to have someone else take this burden off your hands. A professional cleaning service will leave your home move-in ready. You can research services online or through referrals. Pricing is typically based on square footage and required cleaning time.

I make sure to let my clients know that it is their responsibility to gather the driver's contact information and walk through the house to confirm that everything has been placed on the truck before it pulls away. At this crazy point of the day, it is important for you to stay focused. The cleaning crew that you hired will be arriving, your neighbors may be coming over to say good-bye, and the moving crew is sitting in their truck ready to pull away. On one of our moves after the truck pulled away, I went back into our home to discover two kitchen cabinets full of spices and baking goods. On another move, I went back into the house and discovered a tall potted silk tree sitting in our foyer. I know that these items seem obvious, but it can be quite surprising how easily the biggest items can be overlooked at this very chaotic time.

Tipping the driver and his moving crew is another item to consider. I personally feel that it is good etiquette to show your appreciation by tipping your movers. You are entrusting all your valued belongings to this crew. As a basic rule of thumb, the industry standard of tipping is based on 5% of the cost of the move. We typically pay half of our cash tip to the lead supervisor or truck driver, and the other half of our cash tip is divided among the moving crew.

See You Soon!

Growing up, I enjoyed watching *The Carol Burnett Show*, which debuted in 1967. At the end of every show, she would sing her well-known theme song: "I'm so glad we had this time together, just to have a laugh or sing a song. Seems we just get started and before you know it, comes the time we have to say, 'so long.'" As I look back as an adult, this song makes me sad. At some point in every phase of our life, it seems like we just get started and then it comes the time we say "so long."

Throughout this stage of moving, I warn my clients that they will be saying a lot of good-byes. *Good-bye* is a word that sounds so final and so permanent. I personally prefer to say "see you soon!" In my heart, my priority is to maintain relationships with all my family and friends, no matter the distance. The sad part is that not all those people left behind are able hold the same commitment. This is an "out of sight, out of mind" scenario. From the perspective of the person moving, it can appear that those people who remain seem to easily return to their busy, nonstop routines as soon as your moving truck pulls away. I can recall the feeling of being forgotten at a time when I most needed to be remembered. One way to take away the pain of feeling forgotten is to take advantage of our world of communication technology. Encourage your friends and family to frequently post pictures and keep you informed of what is happening in their lives. Social media can take away the miles and provide a comforting lifeline when you are in an unknown world surrounded by strangers.

Along with farewells comes going-away parties. Over the years, I have shared with my clients that I am not such a big fan of these social gatherings. While it's fun to eat cake and enjoy conversation, somehow pulling everyone together under these circumstances only provides a reminder of everything that is being left behind. In fact, our sons have come home from their farewell parties feeling even more sad and discouraged than before they went. These parties are not necessarily a happy experience for those who are moving. The last couple times we moved, I requested that we not have any formal gatherings labeled "going away." In my experience, I have found that meeting friends or family for coffee or a meal was much more enjoyable and not near as overwhelming during this transitional period.

I advise my clients that one of the best ways to raise their spirits at this time of separation is to mark their calendar with dates that they will be available to return home for a visit and to schedule dates that visitors can come see them. When we left our son and his wife behind in Tennessee, it felt better to say "see you soon" knowing that we would be seeing them in only four weeks. Focusing on the future instead of looking at the past feels more encouraging for everyone involved.

Step 5

Your New Address

This is the point where I encourage my clients to "hang in there!" You have finally arrived at your destination, living in limbo out of a suitcase and feeling very unsettled. Give yourself credit for the accomplishments you have made. While you may be uncomfortable with your new surroundings, physically fatigued from the actual move, and emotionally weighed down, you are successfully surviving one of the greatest life-changing events that you will ever encounter.

Move-In Ready

Once you have finalized all the closing documents and received the keys, it will be time to prepare to move into your new home. Before the moving truck arrives, take some time to get your home move-in ready. Depending on the gap between closing and moving into your house, there are some tasks that I suggest my clients consider. It would be a good idea to keep track of these items in your moving binder.

- Establish utilities (telephone, gas, electric, water, cable, Internet).
- Be aware that you may need a television on site when the cable is installed.
- Hire a professional service to clean your home. Focus on cabinets, shelves, appliances, and bathrooms.
- Paint the interior of the home to coordinate with your furnishings or to neutralize colors.
- Professionally clean or replace carpets.

- Professionally repair, clean, and buff hardwood floors.
- Professionally service and clean the heating and air conditioning units.
- Professionally clean the dryer vent and chimney to prevent a fire hazard.
- Hire a pest control service to treat the home.
- Replace old toilets or toilet seat lids. Stock the bathrooms with toilet paper, soap, and towels.
- Replace light bulbs and clean the fixtures.
- Wash window interiors and exteriors.
- Install temporary shades or coverings on windows for privacy.
- Place rugs and protective coverings on the floor to avoid tracking and scratches.
- Shovel the driveway and sidewalks if it has been snowing and sprinkle ice melt.
- Change the locks on exterior doors.
- Change the garage-door opener code.

Move-In Day

Move-in day is very similar to move-out day, except it is in reverse order. Please refer back to Step 4 for a refresher.

- Park your vehicles down the street away from your driveway.
- Stock the refrigerator with bottled water and snacks for you and the moving crew.
- Determine the location of furniture, specifically beds and larger items.
- Label rooms so that the moving crew will understand where to place boxes.
- Have cash available for tipping the cleaning crew, delivery services, and the moving crew.
- Lock your purse or valuables in your vehicle. Keep your checkbook available.
- Refer to your moving binder for delivery appointments and contact numbers.
- Maintain access to your portable office box (computer, chargers, pen, paper).
- Keep your camera available to take pictures of broken or damaged items for future moving claims.

Once the truck is unloaded, make sure that all your furniture and heavy items are positioned to your liking. I encourage my clients to take advantage of their available manpower and reposition furniture or boxes prior to their moving crew's departure. Otherwise, they may be left with items that will be too difficult to move on their own. Typically the movers assemble the beds, tables, and furniture that were disassembled prior to being loaded on the truck. All the required hardware pieces for your furniture can conveniently be located in the miscellaneous parts box that was created prior to the move.

Unpacking and Organizing

Your once empty house has now become a sea of boxes. It can feel quite overwhelming to anticipate the labor-intensive project that now sits before you. At this point, I assure my clients that for every personal belonging that they unpack, they will begin to feel one step closer to being settled.

The first boxes to locate are your first-night survival boxes. Making every bed and pulling out your basic necessities will prepare you for your first night in your new home. This would also be a good time to unpack the family suitcases and settle in for the night. It always feels good to regain your own bed, pillow, blankets, and personal items.

I personally feel that the kitchen boxes take the most time to unpack. If you have assistance, or have hired the moving company to help you unpack, the kitchen would be the perfect place to begin. Take a look at your cabinets and get a feel for how you will best operate in your kitchen. I prefer to place the dishes and glassware near the sink and dishwasher. All the pots, pans, and cooking accessories can be placed near the stove, oven, and microwave. I have found that in the midst of the chaos, I go ahead and place everything in the drawers and cabinets. Down the road, once you have an opportunity to spend some time in your kitchen, you can reorganize the space to best accommodate your needs.

Of course, my husband's first priority is to unpack the electronics! His goal is to have the televisions up and running before the first big football or basketball game begins! The sooner you can get your children's gaming systems and electronic entertainment established, the sooner you will have uninterrupted time to unpack.

As your time and energy allows, continue unpacking room by room according to your needs. Sometimes taking a break to go out for dinner or even to run to the grocery store can give you renewed energy to dig back into the boxes. As each box is unpacked, flatten and stack the boxes in the garage or even outside on your patio. Keep some larger boxes assembled to stuff moving paper and recyclable trash in. I warn my clients to make sure that every box is completely empty prior to stuffing moving paper back into the box. On one of our moves, my husband misplaced his wallet. To this day, we feel that the wallet was accidentally stuffed along with packing paper into a load of boxes that were taken to the dump. Once you have completed the majority of the unpacking, contact your moving company to pick up the pile of boxes and packing paper.

Hair, Health, Hobbies, and Homework

Finding a new physician, dentist, or health club can be difficult. But personally, I feel the most challenging service to locate is the right person to color and cut my hair! Sometimes, this alone is a good enough reason not to move!

Referrals and online research are the best ways to find these services. Remember that you are the customer or patient hiring someone to provide you a professional service. This is a trial-and-error situation that has no deadlines. It may take a few visits before you know if the relationship is a good fit. You can always continue with your search if you are not satisfied.

When I was in sales and marketing, I became accustom to conducting "cold calls" with my customers. The same concepts can be utilized during this evaluation process. Simply walk into the business or office of the specialty you are seeking, greet the receptionist with a friendly smile, explain your situation, then gather a business card and write some notes on the back. You will be amazed how quickly you can gain information just by previewing the waiting room and talking with the staff.

Hair

The best way to find a qualified hair stylist is by referral. Look around town, find a person with good-looking hair, and ask her where she goes for a haircut! I have been known to stop people in the grocery store or at church to compliment them on their hair. People are usually flattered by your kind words and are more than willing to share the referral. Make note of the name of the salon along with the name of the particular stylist that was recommended. You can personally contact the salon for pricing, services, and hours.

I have also found it helpful to interview stylists by booking an appointment for a shampoo and blowout. Spending some time in the salon allows you to make note of its cleanliness, types of products utilized, experience of stylists, and availability of appointments. Talking with a stylist under these circumstances is less of a commitment than hiring someone cold turkey to perform a more in-depth procedure. Even if you decide that this particular person is not the right fit for your needs, you will have your hair styled for a night out on the town!

Another idea is to ask the concierge at a high-end hotel about the hair stylists that they utilize. Hotels frequently have a list of stylists that work with bridal parties or other special events in the hotel. If a bride is happy with her stylist, you may be happy, too!

Health

Besides asking people that you meet for physician referrals, local hospitals can provide referral services, too. Your medical, dental, and vision insurance coverage will determine which physicians are in your network.

Once you have the name of a physician to evaluate, make an appointment for an annual physical or even a blood-pressure check. This appointment will allow you time to determine if the clinic and physician will meet your needs. The same process can work with finding a dentist. I have scheduled six-month dental checkups and even a teeth cleaning just to have the opportunity to meet with a dentist and hygienist. This face-to-face contact gives valuable insight and information.

Once you have acquired a physician, they will be able to give you recommendations for other qualified specialties that you may be seeking. Keep in mind that before registering your children for a new school, especially if you have moved out of state, all required vaccination and health records for each student need to be updated by a local medical professional.

Hobbies

Whether you are researching arts and crafts, music, or a golf club membership, the Internet is a great resource. When you are new to a city, utilizing search engines such as Google can connect you and your family with many new hobbies and extracurricular activities.

Finding a fitness club may be one of those activities. The first step is to take some time to preview and compare a few gyms that are convenient to your home or office. Typically, gyms will offer a trial period to try out the facility prior to committing to a membership. During this timeframe, you can determine if the facility is clean and professionally operated and has well-maintained equipment. This timeframe will also give you the opportunity to review the gym's membership offers, policies, hours, and classes prior to signing any contracts.

The parks and recreation department of your city is also a good resource for various activities. They can provide a calendar of local events including upcoming sporting lessons, race events, holiday events, and entertainment. The recreation department can also provide registration information and deadlines for sporting leagues and teams for adults as well as children. Some other organizations you may pursue are youth sports leagues such as a youth football or softball association.

Homework

When I think of homework, I think of school. There are several items to consider when getting your children prepared for their new school. Each state varies on its requirements, so I encourage my clients to research the county in which they are residing. If your child will be attending a private school, the first step will be to complete the school's application and enrollment process.

- **School registration packet.** Stop by the school or go to their website to acquire the necessary paperwork and list of documents required for registration. Some documents that you may need to provide are your child's birth certificate, proof of residency, affidavit of residence, social security number, academic records, immunization certificate, and ear-eye-dental screening.
- **School calendar.** This is usually located on the county website within the school zone in which you are living. This calendar can be helpful for determining the first and last days of school, teacher workdays, as well as student breaks and holidays. It is also important to research the county's inclement weather policies to determine when and how school closing announcements are broadcast.
- **New student orientation.** Some schools offer a new student orientation prior to the first day of school. This session can be

quite beneficial, allowing new students to become familiar with their school by reviewing a map and actually walking the hallways. A big area of concern is acquiring a locker and learning the combination.

- **Dress code.** Find out what the students are required to wear to school every day. Is there a specific uniform that needs to be purchased or a general dress code to be followed? This may require a shopping trip or a uniform order online. This is also a good time to inquire about the gym clothes requirements.
- **Lunch.** Food is a priority for our kids! I encourage my clients to research, prior to their child's first day of school, how lunch and snacks are purchased. Do students need to establish meal account cards? Can they bring their own lunch? Are students allowed to bring a snack to class?

  Lunchtime can be a confusing time in a school cafeteria. One of the biggest fears of a new student is sitting alone to eat lunch. I suggest to my clients that they talk with the school staff regarding this concern. Elementary and middle schools typically assign a current student to serve as a companion to a new student. Coordinating a lunch companion for a high school student can be more difficult, since course schedules vary among students. I asked my son Andrew about this situation, and he personally found it helpful to find a student from the class prior to lunch that was walking to the cafeteria at the same time. My older son, Adam, told me, several years following his high school graduation, that the first several weeks at his new high school were so awkward and uncomfortable that he would hide in the bathroom just to pass the time.
- **Fees.** Get your checkbook ready! Between books, school supplies, athletic passes, lockers, combination locks, and parking permits, enrolling your child in school can be quite costly.
- **Transportation.** A school bus routing schedule will be posted on your county website. Before your child's first day of school, talk with your new neighbors to confirm the exact timing and location of the bus pickup and drop-off. If you are personally driving your child to school, review the school's carpool protocol.
- **Medication and special medical needs.** It would be a good idea to talk with the school nurse prior to your children's first day of school if they have any health issues or allergies or require medication that needs to be administered daily. Every school has different policies and procedures.

- **Parent teacher organization (PTO).** This organization consists of parents, teachers, and school staff. This is a good group to join when you are a new parent and you want to volunteer in school fund-raising and encourage teachers and students.
- **Extracurricular activities.** Being a new student is very difficult. You are going to be key in encouraging your children to become involved in their school activities, clubs, or sports. While you don't want them to become overcommitted, these groups will be the best way to start the process of building new friendships.

Department of Motor Vehicles

Why is it that we feel a sense of intimidation when we think about the Department of Motor Vehicles? Are we fearful that our independence will be taken away if we do not successfully pass our written drivers test? Do we dread the thought of standing in long lines for hours while feeling uncertain that we are holding the correct paperwork and required documentation? Are we saddened by the fact that we are relinquishing one more aspect of our previous life by acquiring a driver's license in a new state? I can personally say "yes" to all these questions. Every time we move to a new home, my concerns surrounding the DMV seem to resurface.

Every state varies on its driver's license application process, change-of-address requirements, and vehicle registration guidelines. I encourage my clients to refer to the new residents guide listed on the Department of Motor Vehicles website (www.dmv.org) prior to making a trip to their local DMV office. This website can provide DMV locations, hours, appointment availability, fees, and required documentation. Depending on your state, you may be able to make changes online or possibly print and complete forms prior to your visit. Voter registration can also be completed at the same time.

If you have crossed state lines and are applying for a driver's license in another state, you need to research the regulations accordingly. In some states, such as Tennessee and Georgia, you will be required to surrender your out-of-state driver's license, pass a vision screening, and provide required documentation. On the other hand, states such as California and Indiana will require the same items along with passing a written test. Just the word *test* can make my blood pressure soar! In fact, one of the first questions that I research when I discover that we are relocating is "Will I be required to take another written drivers test?"

If you are a procrastinator, I can understand why you would want to avoid rushing into the Department of Motor Vehicles to update your driver's license and vehicle registration. However, in order for your personal contact information to be correct, I highly recommend that you make this step a priority. If for some reason you should have a medical emergency or experience a car accident, it would be extremely difficult for the authorities to locate your loved ones if your personal identification information is not current. Another reason to make this step a priority is that some states require you to register your vehicle within twenty days of establishing residency. The last thing you need at this hectic time is to be given a ticket with heavy penalties because of procrastination.

Insurance is another important item to address when you relocate. Contact your insurance agent to update your automobile coverage and liability insurance. A lot of factors are taken into consideration in your insurance package.

Take a Break

The stress and anxiety surrounding a move require an escape from reality. Just a change of routine and scenery can help you recharge. This much needed break can actually provide health and psychological benefits for the entire family.

Ideally, in order to totally relax, set aside a few days for a break that will physically remove you from your normal day-to-day surroundings. I have found that as long as I remain at home, I will continue to work. There is something about not checking e-mails or listening to voicemail messages that can temporarily relieve the burden of daily responsibilities.

We have had periods during our moving transitions that we have been placed in a "holding pattern" while our home was being built or we were waiting on our home to close. This is a good time to squeeze in a break. We have also had times that we took advantage of the time we had between our move-in day and the first day of beginning a new school. I encourage my clients to escape from their house full of unpacked boxes for a week to give them renewed energy that will allow them to return fully recharged.

I encourage my clients to take some kind of vacation from their moving routine, even if it's only for a day. The key is to get away and have some fun. This can involve a leisure activity such as golfing, boating, or even shopping! Just an outing to the movies or eating a sit-down lunch could suffice. Your children may enjoy going to a local theme park, taking a hike, or spending the day at the beach. You may also enjoy using this time to research activities that your new city may offer. Having some time to talk about anything other than moving, leaving friends, expenses, and new schools will provide you with a well-deserved break.

Step 6

"I Want to Go Home!"

At this point, the excitement of the move is starting to fade, and the reality of your new life begins to become clear. I tell my clients that there will be days that you are thrilled with your fresh new adventure and then days that you will want to run for the hills. This feeling reminds me of the Michael Bublé song "Let Me Go Home": "May be surrounded by a million people, I still feel all alone. I just wanna go home." Going back home to your comfort zone may just feel like the best solution to the heavy emotional adjustment that you are experiencing.

Moving Emotions

When I was in college, I took a course on loss and grief. We studied the five stages of the grieving process that Elisabeth Kubler-Ross addressed in her 1969 book *On Death and Dying.*

When we speak about grieving, we often think of death. However, loss can occur in every aspect of life, including illness, divorce, or even a relocation. People as a whole can't imagine the grief and loss that can be suffered by those who relocate. Transitioning from a life full of familiarity into a life full of unfamiliarity can stir a magnitude of emotions. Throughout your move, you may experience Kubler-Ross's five stages of the grieving process, which I describe in the paragraphs that follow. You will find that you can easily drift back and forth between the stages in the matter of hours, days, weeks, or even years.

Denial is the stage when you allow your mind to go numb. It is less painful to avoid the reality of what is really happening. Denial is when you may say, "No, I am not moving," "I can't believe we are moving," or "I thought we would live in the house until our children were grown."

You may find yourself not wanting to discuss the move. You may feel as though you don't want to face questions to which you have no answers. Denial is like the calm before the storm. Until you are ready to pull out the umbrella and the rubber boots, you just don't want to go out into the rain.

Anger is the stage where you start feeling the pain of your moving reality. I explain to my clients that anger can manifest as frustration and may unintentionally get displaced randomly toward others at work, people in traffic, or whomever just so happens to be standing right in front of them! You may be angry with your spouse, or even his boss, for putting you through this painful experience. You may find yourself angry with those around you that are happily going along with their comfortable, uninterrupted lives.

Sometimes your family and friends will express their sadness as anger toward you. It's important for you to understand that they, too, are sad that you will be leaving a void in their lives. This is a difficult predicament, because at the time when you most need comfort and encouragement from others, they will need your emotional support. This in turn can make you feel angry that your personal crisis does not take priority over their emotions.

Anger can also stir up as other people express doubt regarding your decision to move. They may question why your spouse doesn't just get another job or why you don't just adjust your lifestyle. At times, you may feel disheartened knowing that your relocation is the topic of every friend's conversation around town.

Bargaining is when you try to change or postpone the inevitable. At this stage, the move is going to occur, and you just try to lessen the pain. I have found that my clients at this stage delay putting their house on the market, announcing their move, or giving notice to their employers.

Depression is the profound sadness that overcomes you when you realize on a deep level that the move is really happening. Nothing is normal anymore as you disassemble your life piece by piece. At this point, you are letting go of more than you are gaining. You think about how much you enjoy your home, relationships, and the life you have built. You may find yourself focusing on your "firsts" as you recall the first time you decorated your home for the holidays or your child's first steps that they took in your home. You may also pay attention to your "lasts," such as this being the last time your family will experience boating on your favorite lake.

Depression is also when we feel regrets for lost opportunities. I can recall feeling sad that we wouldn't be living in the same town as our newlywed son Adam and his wife, Anna. I grieved the fact that we would not live near future grandchildren. I was sad that my younger son, Andrew, would not grow up close to his older brother. How we would miss birthday parties with our friends, dropping in at our parents' house for an impromptu dinner, or having my same OB-GYN deliver my future children.

Acceptance is reaching the stage of peace surrounding all the changes that will be occurring in your life. This is where you begin to focus on the things ahead of you instead of the things left behind you. You find an appreciation for what has been gained in life, and while your future may look different, that doesn't mean that it can't be bright and successful. I tell my clients that they may never fully accept everything about their relocation, but gradually they will accept one piece at a time. It was not difficult for me to accept the gorgeous year-round weather in Southern California, but I never fully accepted the two-thousand-mile distance that separated us from our loved ones.

Acceptance is when you stop comparing your new life to your old life. While you may miss the people, weather, food, and daily routines, you can still find happiness with new traditions and friendships. Allow yourself to embrace change, and don't feel guilty about enjoying the experiences. I know that I have personally reached acceptance when I feel a total calm and peace. The memories of today will be the ones that you may grieve once time has taken this day away. Live for today and look forward to new experiences tomorrow. As Maya Angelou once said, "Be present in all things and thankful for all things."

Adjusting with Children

Every time we move, I feel like I am re-experiencing childbirth! We can have several days pass smoothly with very little pain. Then, all of a sudden, we have a tough day, and a major labor contraction occurs! The German philosopher Friedrich Nietzsche made the eloquent statement "That which does not kill us, makes us stronger." I can say from my experience that at times I have felt like we were killing our children. I named this book *It's Not Just about the Boxes* because I personally feel that moving is 30% about the boxes, and the other 70% is all about our emotions!

I tell my clients that the age of their children can affect how quickly they will adjust to a new home, school, and city. No matter the age of your children, there will difficult days. New bedrooms, jobs, routines, schools, emotions, tryouts, birthdays, holidays, and relationships can all contribute to the painful labor!

During the elementary school years, parents are allowed to be more involved in helping their children rebuild their social calendar. New friendships can be formed through sports, gymnastics, music, or any social activity that the parent has control of registering their child for. At this age, their school is always requesting volunteers, and this opportunity provides more hands-on control in arranging playdates and talking with other children's parents. Younger children also seem to be more open to adding new friends to their already existing groups. As our children move into adolescence, the rules to the relationship game begin to change.

Dealing with emotions, peer pressure, and self-confidence during the adolescent years can be tough. At this time of life, where predictability is most important, you are asking your teenager to leave the familiarity of their friends, family, and home. To a teenager, starting all over and rebuilding their life can seem unfathomable. As a relocation specialist, I work with people who can't cope well with this experience as adults, much less as self-conscious teenagers. In this situation, parents have limited opportunities to be a part of their teen's social circle. Activity choices become more limited, and only those who successfully survive a tough tryout regimen will be placed on a sports team. The reassurance of love, safety, and security from parents, siblings, and mentors is crucial.

- **Use teamwork.** There is strength in numbers. I have told my sons that while this experience will be difficult, we will stick together as a team, and with God as our leader, we can get through anything. "For where two or three are gathered in my name, there am I in the midst of them" (Matthew 18:20). Sometimes, just knowing that they are not alone can have a great impact on your children's journey.
- **Focus on the positive.** Exciting adventures, career opportunities, and a lot of happiness is ahead of you. While you may not see all the wonderful things just yet, some great life experiences

are just around the corner. Having a positive attitude can show your children that it is not what happens to them in life but how they react to life's ups and downs that will matter the most.

- **Encourage, encourage, encourage!** Need I say more? You are your child's best cheerleader. I can recall about four months into one of our moves when our son Andrew said, "I really thought by now that I would have a friend." He felt defeated, and it was my role to encourage him to stay in the game. I strongly believe that God chooses each of us to accomplish great things if we are willing to surrender to His plan. Do we stay where we are comfortable and always wonder what we missed, or do we endure life's uncomfortable moments, fasten our seatbelts, and go for the ride?
- **Pray.** Praying allows us to place our burdens in the hands of God. Prayer is very therapeutic and has the power to reduce stress and worry. When we pray, we open the lines of communication with our heavenly father. As our children face the daily challenges of our move, the opportunity to pray with you will allow them to gain courage and strength through calling on God.
- **Cry.** Moving is a grieving process, and it needs to be treated as one. Let your children know that it is normal to be sad and to cry during difficult times. About one week after my son started at his new high school, he came home with tears in his eyes as he told me that he had eaten lunch by himself that day. These are the words that every mother fears the most. This comment allowed both of us to sit together and cry over the reality of the situation. Being vulnerable is one of the best ways to grow closer with your children during this difficult time.
- **Build social networks.** To a teenager who is already feeling like an outsider, social networking tools can sometime hurt more than help. I know that our sons have built their lives around these communication tools. Between Instagram, Snapchat, Facebook, and Twitter, they are able to immediately stay informed of events. There is nothing worse, however, than receiving a photograph from your best friends when they appear to be having such a good time without you. It can feel like life went on without skipping a beat when you left town. This can be a catch-22 situation. No matter which way you go, there is going to be an undesired result or outcome. Our teenagers get torn, because they want to communicate with their old friends because they miss them, yet

they don't want to communicate with their old friends because they fear that life has gone on without them.

- **Listen.** I encourage my clients to stop unpacking those boxes and give their children full attention when they start talking about their concerns. Let them fully express their point of view, both good and bad. They want to feel heard even if you don't provide a solution to their problem. They need to release their burdens to someone who is truly listening.
- **Participate in extracurricular activities.** The sooner your children start feeling connected to their new environment, the better they will feel about their new home. Golf and skateboarding were the sports that saved our sons during our moves. These activities gave them a personal challenge and were a good way to burn off built-up energy. Focusing on a sport or personal interest can help your children until they determine the place that they best fit within their new community.

Facing Loneliness

It is normal to feel isolated after moving to a new area. I tell my clients that being cut off or disconnected from family, friends, and meaningful relationships can cause great loneliness. I have had friends tell me that they cannot even consider moving or allowing their spouse to take a job promotion out of town, because of their powerful fear of anticipated loneliness.

The truth is, whether you move or not, everyone will experience lonely chapters of life. Some of the loneliest people can be in a room full of people and yet still feel very isolated. The Beatles are famous for the song "Eleanor Rigby," also known as "All the Lonely People," which addresses all the lonely people and where they belong. As much as we want to avoid loneliness, we will all face it, and learning ways to overcome this powerful, empty feeling of isolation is key.

After several years of moving and spending time alone, I have found that it's not the end of the world to be your own best friend. I know that this sounds like being such a loser, but it really is the truth. I can recall years of striving to place myself into social settings constantly surrounded by people. I don't know if this was because I was raised in a home of six family members and never really had the opportunity to be alone or if I am such a people person that I felt my best by not allowing myself to be alone.

Relocating has taught me that isolation and time alone can be a positive thing. Don't get me wrong: adjusting to being alone is an extremely difficult process that takes time, but learning how to be your own best companion can bring you freeing independence. I encourage my clients to give themselves permission to embrace this chapter of their life. Stay open to the positive aspects of being by yourself, and don't fight the fear of isolation. Quietness allows you to see the blessings of day-to-day life, to hear the beauty of music, and to smell the freshness of blooming flowers and sea air.

- Regardless of my address, God is my friend that is always by my side. All I have to do is simply love Him, listen to Him for guidance, and have faith that He will never leave me. Listening to spiritual music and inspirational messages on podcasts, along with studying scripture, significantly fills my lonely surroundings.
- Pet therapy is very effective when you feel lonely. I have found that the unconditional love and companionship of my golden retriever has taken a tremendous amount of loneliness away from our quiet home. In fact, I trained Rainey to become a therapy dog so that I could take her nurturing gift to others who may be experiencing loneliness. Walking your dog is another route to open up your isolated world. There is something about the non-threatening aspect of a pet that allows people to begin a casual conversation with a total stranger.
- I truly enjoy going to the movies. Growing older, I have determined that it is all right to go see a movie all by myself. There are times that I have taken advantage of the time that my children were at school to go see a matinee. I have found myself feeling a freeing sense of independence from the grips of my loneliness by taking a couple of hours to experience someone else's life through film.
- Leaving the isolation of your home can place you into a world of people and activity. Running errands or going to the beauty salon, mall, or a place of worship can remove you from the feeling that you are all alone. I have found that talking to the attendant at the dry cleaners, or a fellow customer in the checkout lane at the grocery store, lightens the weight of the quietness. I have even laughed to myself that the voice on my Garmin GPS gives me companionship just instructing me around town while preventing me from getting lost.

- Take yourself on a date! Grab a good book and spend the afternoon sitting at Barnes & Noble people watching. Take your laptop out for lunch! Enjoy free Wi-Fi while eating at an outdoor restaurant. Don't be afraid that everyone around you will be looking at you like you are a lonely loser. In all actuality, onlookers will probably be envious of your "me time"!
- Social media can provide a feeling of being connected even in a world where you feel very unconnected. Sending and receiving messages along with photographs makes me feel included in the day-to-day lives of my family and friends who live many miles away.
- Write a book! I was able to turn my periods of quietness into creative and productive opportunities to share my personal life-relocation experience through writing this book.

The Guilt of the Breadwinner

It can be quite exciting to be given a promotion or a new job assignment, but sometimes taking a new role requires the family to relocate. The person taking the new assignment can be left with tremendous guilt. Knowing that he or she is the one responsible for his or her loved ones' future and happiness is a heavy burden. The truth of the matter is that whether you are the one taking the promotion or the one supporting the situation, everyone involved will experience a roller coaster of emotions swaying from the highs of excitement to the lows of fear.

I stress to my clients that being the main breadwinner of the family can be a big responsibility. There is a lot of pressure on that person to not only succeed in their career but also succeed as a leader of the family. An uncertain, constantly changing economy requires flexibility even if it means relocating to a new city. It is important for everyone to understand that being the "cause" of the move is a very heavy burden to carry.

Going Back to Visit

I prefer to wait until my children have had an opportunity to adjust to their new routine before returning back home for a visit. I tell my clients that it is important to their kids' adjustment to spend a significant amount of time at their new school, with new activities and friends, before returning to the life that they left. The truth of the matter is that time is the only factor that can make things better. Upon their return back home, they will have both good and bad comments to share, but at least they can take ownership of their own opinions. The more answers they have regarding their new life, the better.

Sometimes just placing a return visit on the calendar can help the adjustment process. Talking about what we are going to do, where we are going to eat, and whom we are going to visit can be therapeutic in its own way. You will find yourself talking with people about your upcoming trip, and the anticipation creates an excitement that can lift everyone's spirits.

Part of the healing process is for the family to be able to revisit their previous lives. I have found, more often than not, that on the first return visits, my boys immediately want to move back. We typically revisit the tears and emotions of when we originally left. This can be very difficult for everyone involved, but I tell my clients that these emotions are to be expected. It has been said that time heals all wounds. While they may never overcome the pain of losing daily contact with their closest family and friends, they will be able to move forward once they have had time to rebuild their life.

Home for the Holidays

As we grow older, our holidays begin to look different. As hard as we may try, it is impossible to totally recreate the memories of the past. This can be especially true if you have moved and are living in a new home. Just like grieving the loss of a loved one during the holidays, you are also grieving the loss of celebrations of the past.

Being away from family and friends during the holidays is difficult. While you sit in the quietness of your new home, you can't help but wonder what you are missing. I can recall walking around our new neighborhood on Thanksgiving Day and seeing all our neighbors' driveways full of cars. All their families and friends were walking into their homes with covered dishes ready for a full day of food and football. Yet we were all alone. Just hearing the Bing Crosby song "I'll Be Home for Christmas" left me with a heavy feeling in my heart.

On the flip side, it gets complicated traveling home for the holidays. It is quite challenging to load the car with gifts, live out of a suitcase, and keep a tight visitation schedule balanced. Meeting everyone else's holiday expectations can be tough. Over the years, it would sadden me that our boys couldn't awaken from their own beds on Christmas morning. How I would have loved to see them run to their own tree and see the brightly wrapped gifts that Santa had brought down their chimney. Only people who have moved can really relate to the difficulty of this situation.

I stress to my clients that moving is a good time to start new holiday traditions. Just because things are different doesn't mean they can't be fun. Sometimes your new traditions can be even more enjoyable than the old ones. While we were living in California, we started a new Thanksgiving Day tradition by eating dinner overlooking the Pacific Ocean. The Fourth of July can be as enjoyable at the ocean as at the lake. There are no rules to setting your own traditions. I believe that as the years pass, you will look back fondly at the wonderful holiday memories you experienced, even though you had moved to a new city.

Step 7

The Next Chapter

Like everything else in life, it takes time to adjust to changes, and the strongest step is the willingness to be open to change. It is important to give yourself permission to take time to adjust to your new home without the pressure of feeling comfortable right away. I have found that the first year in your new home allows you to experience each season for the first time. The second year starts to become easier as you begin repeating some of the routines from the previous year. By the third year, life starts to fall into place. You will never forget your old life, but the sting of your move will fade with each passing day.

Employment Considerations

During the first twenty-five years of my marriage, I worked full-time. Every time my husband was promoted in his career and we relocated, I was also required to relocate my career. Luckily, since I was in a sales position, my company was able to transfer my employment to a new territory near our new home. The majority of the time, it is necessary for the breadwinner's significant other to find employment once they are settled. Either way, it can get quite complicated to balance two new jobs in a strange city, especially if children are involved.

I tell my clients that it is a good practice to keep their resume updated along with a portfolio of career accomplishments and professional recommendations. Depending on your area of expertise, referrals may be available within your industry. Recruiters, online job postings, and job placement specialists are key to finding employment.

Since finding a job is a whole other book, I am going to refer you to the experts in the employment arena.

What I can inform you about is the fact that balancing a full-time job, family, and home in a new city is the ultimate challenge in the area of multitasking. Since I do have experience in this area, I have listed some items to consider if you have children and are considering employment opportunities in your new city.

- Consider waiting to purchase your home until you have determined the logistics of your daily commute to and from your new job. You may decide to purchase a home on a different side of town.
- Research childcare options. Enrollment waiting lists can get quite lengthy at top-rated childcare centers and preschools. What is your alternative plan until space becomes available at the school of your choice? What are your elementary-age childcare options before and after school? Does the school or a local recreation center provide childcare or sports camps over the days before and after major holidays? Are there special programs offered during fall, winter, spring, and summer breaks? Overall, consider the cost of childcare throughout the year. Rates can get quite pricey, and sometimes it just doesn't pay to work outside of the home.
- Research school transportation. How are the children in the neighborhood being transported to and from school? Does the school system provide transportation? What are your transportation options if your children are enrolled in a private school? What are your transportation options for afterschool functions and sporting events?
- Take a look at your work hours and flexibility. Will you be working full-time or part-time? How flexible are your work hours? What is your plan if your child gets sick or school is cancelled due to inclement weather? Who will care for your children in the summer when school is out of session? Will you be required to travel out of town for work assignments or job training?

I know that this list can look quite daunting, but I do know that everything seems to fall into place as you work through the process. Networking is key to finding assistance with the transportation and care of your children. A college student or a neighbor may be looking for additional income and may end up being the answer to your prayers.

Build a Social Calendar

This is a time in life when you actually may have an empty calendar. You may have gone from a life that barely had a minute free to a life that has practically every minute free! I tell my clients that filling their daily calendar is their first step toward becoming socially busy. This is a time when you need to step out of your comfort zone and initiate some action. You may need to be the one to offer the invitation instead of waiting for an invitation.

Hospitality

- Invite neighbors over for a barbecue.
- Host a ladies coffee or Bunco.
- Join the neighborhood social committee.
- Invite someone you meet to join you for lunch, shopping, or a movie.
- Volunteer to welcome newcomers.

Fitness

- Ask a neighbor to go walking with you regularly.
- Join a gym or an exercise class.
- Sign up to train with a group for a marathon.
- Bike or hike in the park.
- Walk your dog.
- Join a golf or tennis league.

Personal Development

- Take a cooking or photography class.
- Register for a bible study course.
- Give back to your community; visit those who are lonely.
- Continue your education at a local college or online.
- Tutor or teach; use your talents to develop others.

Create Personal Calling Cards

When I worked in the corporate world, I gave my customers a business card so that they would have my contact information. I have adopted this same concept when I move to a new city by creating my own personal calling cards. These personalized cards are inexpensive and can be ordered conveniently online. On each card, I include my name, telephone number, and e-mail address. Handing your personal information on a calling card is so much easier than trying to quickly locate piece of paper and a pen. I encourage my clients to keep a few of these cards available to share as needed with someone such as a new neighbor, painter, home repair service, or a potential new friend.

I have found that actually mailing new address cards through the US Postal Service is more effective than e-mailing this information out to family and friends. Everyone seems to more efficiently update their contact information when they receive an actual card. These cards can also be ordered online through www.tinyprints.com, www.vistaprint.com, or www.zazzle.com, or you can design your own cards on your personal computer.

At this time, I also order a return address stamp and address labels. There is something about seeing your name with your new address that can make you feel more connected to your new home.

Make New Friends

Can you remember in high school when you started to date? I can recall feeling nervous, uncomfortable, and fearful of being rejected. Building new friendships is very similar to the world of dating. Finding compatible companions who can share your common interests and life experiences requires time, memories, loyalty, and respect. There is no way to rush the process, regardless of how quickly you would like it to happen. This may be a good time to refer back to Step 1, where I discussed adjusting your attitude, specifically in the areas of patience and faith.

When you move to a new city, you will need to step out of your comfort zone and remain open minded to the variety of people you will encounter. In reality, you will be attempting to make a place for yourself in another person's life. This is when you do more listening than talking, are more complimentary than critical, and say "yes" to social opportunities even when you would really prefer to say "no."

At the beginning, the majority of the initial relationships that you form will be with acquaintances. These are the people that you talk with on a superficial level as you chat at the grocery store, school, the gym, or work. While acquaintances are great resources for gathering information regarding your new home, school, or city, they will not fill the void of having a close friendship. I like Jay Leno's comment about acquaintances: "Go through your phone book, call people, and ask them to drive you to the airport. The ones who will drive you are your true friends. The rest aren't bad people; they're just acquaintances."

I stress to my clients to not take it personally if people aren't as eager to meet them as they are to meet new people. Remember that people already have established routines and a network of family and friends. I try to give people benefit of the doubt, although I must say it can feel hurtful. We have lived in neighborhoods for years and have rarely seen our next-door neighbors. In one of our homes, I actually had a neighbor stand in my kitchen and tell me that she would never be my friend. Of course, she had been drinking several glasses of wine, but you can only imagine how shocking it was to hear those words. There is nothing you can do about the way people respond to you except to continue to be your authentic self. The best friends are the worth waiting for, even if it takes some time.

New Friendship Expectations

- Don't attempt to duplicate the friendships that you left behind. Every phase of life and every situation will be different. Keep your heart open to the many possibilities of "different-looking" friendships.
- Don't judge others for being their authentic selves. Appreciate the fact that everyone has something to contribute to a friendship.
- Don't attend functions with the sole idea of making friends or meeting people. Try to go with no expectations and enjoy yourself regardless of what happens.

Invest in Friendships

- To have a good friend, you must first be a good friend.
- Putting a smile on someone else's face can take the frown off your face.
- Offer an invitation instead of waiting for others to give you an invitation.
- Keep your ears open to events occurring in someone else's life. Acknowledge special days such as a birthday, anniversary, new baby, or wedding. Express condolences when you hear about a death or job loss. Provide meals, transportation, and emotional support in cases such as a serious illness or injury.

A Vacation Destination

One of the best ways to build memories in your new home is to welcome out-of-town guests. There is something wonderful about filling every room of your new home with love, conversation, and laughter. Unfamiliar surroundings begin to turn into more familiar surroundings with happy memories. It feels good to have one-on-one visit time with those that you have missed, especially at a time when you have not yet developed many new relationships.

If you have relocated somewhere fun, expect lots of company! While we were living in California, I found that my family and friends planned their annual vacation trips to visit us. Once your company has experienced your new surroundings, it will be easier to communicate with them about your new life. I have also found, due to time restraints, that sometimes you get a better overall visit when people come to your home versus when you return back to visit them.

My goal is to make my guests feel at home. A little hospitality and a few extra touches can make your guests feel welcome and special. If you are not accustomed to having overnight guests, I have noted some tips to consider.

- Anticipating the arrival of guests can give you that extra nudge to finish unpacking those final boxes and to get rid of the extra clutter sitting throughout the house. It is also a good time to give your new house a thorough cleaning.
- Ideally, you have an additional room that can be considered a guest room. If this is not an option, your children's bedrooms can also accommodate guests, too. Make sure you have clean sheets, fresh pillows, and extra blankets. Light a candle to make everything smell fresh and welcoming.
- Double-check the guest bathroom for cleanliness prior to their arrival. Buy some new towels for the bathroom instead of using the hand-me-down towels from other bathrooms. It is nice to provide some toiletries like a fresh bar of soap, shampoo, conditioner, and lotion. Place a night light in the hallway leading to the bathroom for guidance in the middle of the night.
- I enjoy providing my guests a little welcome package upon their arrival. Include local tourist brochures, local candy or snacks, along with some bottled water.

Take your visitors to some of your favorite restaurants, shopping malls, or social settings. This is a good time to venture out to areas that you have not seen. There is a lot that can be learned about a city if you look at it from the perspective of a tourist. Take the double-decker city bus tour, attend a concert, or take in a sporting event.

Pay It Forward

We spend so much of our time during the moving process focusing on the leaving portion and very little time pondering the welcoming portion of the process. When we leave the place that we call home, we are surrounded by farewell gatherings and good-bye hugs. But when we arrive to the place that we now call our new home, there is no one to welcome us. I find it quite sad that at a time when we need a hug the most, there is no one available to offer us a hug!

Once you have experienced a move, you will never forget the feelings of vulnerability you experienced as an outsider. This is why it is important for you to reach out to newcomers as they move into your community. As a veteran of relocation, you are the one most familiar with the moving emotions of fear, excitement, loss of identity, grief, and disappointment.

It doesn't take a whole lot of effort to welcome a new family to your neighborhood. Basically, all you have to do is show up! I tell my clients that they have the ability to give the gift of community to someone who may feel very disconnected. Just push yourself out of your comfort zone and help others move into their new comfort zone. There are several Bible verses in the book of Matthew that address being a good neighbor such as "Though shalt love thy neighbor as thyself" and "So in everything, do to others what you would have them do to you." Do what you wish you would have had done for you!

I gain great pleasure from welcoming newcomers. There is nothing better than being greeted with a smile and cookies! My signature welcome goodies are Rice Krispie Treats. Bringing a pot of soup or a tray of sandwiches is great, too. I always include an index card with our names, address, telephone number, e-mail address, and names of our kids with their ages. One of the best feelings, being new to a community, is to have at least one contact name if an emergency should arise. I have also hosted a barbecue for new neighbors to give them the opportunity to meet other new neighbors. Whatever you do will be greatly appreciated.

Conclusion

The process of moving really never ends. There will always be cabinets and closets to Dump, Designate, or Donate. There will always be people leaving your life and new people entering your life. Whether you are moving to a new house or starting a new job, the seven-step process that I have described in this book can be used in every aspect of life. As I always tell my clients, "If you don't go, you will never know!"

The next time you see a moving truck or hear about someone relocating, ponder the words "It's not just about the boxes." Remember all the challenges, emotions, and personal growth you experienced. Remember that there is so much more to a move than boxes, trucks, and aching backs. It's not just the "stuff" we put into boxes and unpack at our new location. It's a journey that impacts our lives and our loves ones in many ways.

CPSIA information can be obtained at www.ICGtesting.com
Printed in the USA
LVOW07s0412230515

439581LV00005BC/294/P